WE BRING
GOOD NEWS

WE BRING GOOD NEWS

A guide to preaching and the celebration of the word

This guide to the celebration of the word was prepared under the auspices of the Irish Commission for Liturgy with the collaboration of Ann Breslin, PhD, SSL, Rev. Billy Fitzgerald, RTE, and A.G. McGrady.

Edited by Brian Gogan CSSp

VERITAS

First published 1989 by
Veritas Publications
7-8 Lower Abbey Street
Dublin 1

Copyright © Brian Gogan 1989

ISBN 1 85390 029 X

Cover design by Eddie McManus
Typesetting by Printset & Design Ltd
Printed in the Republic of Ireland by
Mount Salus Press Ltd

Contents

Foreword

It gives me great pleasure to welcome the publication of *We Bring Good News*.

The task of proclaiming the gospel is central to the life of the Church and a constant challenge to clergy and laity alike.

The Spirit of God, speaking in the post-Vatican II Church, urges the clergy to listen, and be attentive to, the voice of the People of God. It is the great value of this book that its findings and recommendations are based on a detailed and nation-wide survey of the felt needs of the faithful.

'The hungry sheep look up . . .' and it would be to our shame as preachers of the word if the findings and guidelines contained in this volume were not to be availed of to the full.

All whose vocation it is 'to proclaim his word' will find here both a challenge and an inspiration.

I hope this book will be widely used by the clergy, and that it will not only spur them on to aim at the highest standards in preaching but also provide them with the means whereby they can make a notable advance towards this objective.

✠ Tomás Cardinal Ó Fiaich
Armagh, 17 March 1989

Abbreviations

AG	= *Ad gentes divinitus: The Decree on the Church's Missionary Activity*, Vatican II, 1965.
BRC	= *Building and Re-organisation of Churches. Pastoral Directory of the Episcopal Liturgical Commission of Ireland*, Dublin, 1972.
CD	= *Christus Dominus: Decree on the Pastoral Office of Bishops in the Church*, Vatican II, 1965.
CIC	= *Codex iuris canonici: The Code of Canon Law*, London, 1983.
Corish	= Patrick J. Corish, *The Irish Catholic Experience, A Historical Survey*, Dublin, 1986.
DV	= *Dei verbum: The Dogmatic Constitution on Divine Revelation*, Vatican II, 1965.
DVD	= *De verbi Dei*, General Introduction to the Lectionary for Mass (Second Edition) S.C.S.D.W., 21 January 1981.
EN	= *Evangelii nuntiandi: Evangelisation in the Modern World*, Paul VI, 8 December 1975.
Fulfilled	= *Fulfilled in Your Hearing, The Homily in the Sunday Assembly*, The Bishops' Committee on Priestly Life and Ministry, National Conference of Catholic Bishops, Washington, DC, 1982.
GS	= *Gaudium et spes: The Pastoral Constitution on the Church in the Modern World*, Vatican II, 1965.
IGMR	= *Institutio Generalis Missalis Romanae: General Instruction on the Roman Missal*, Rome, 1969.
LG	= *Lumen gentium: The Dogmatic Constitution on the Church*, Vatican II, 1964.
PO	= *Presbyterorum ordinis: Decree on the Ministry and Life of Priests*, Vatican II, 1965.
SC	= *Sacrosanctum concilium: The Constitution on the Sacred Liturgy*, Vatican II, 1963.

Introduction

There are many fine statements in tradition on the subject of preaching, many helpful books, monographs and articles on pastoral liturgy. This guide to the celebration of the word in the Sunday Eucharist takes as its starting point the views and needs of Irish people and their priests. These needs were expressed in response to a survey commissioned by the Irish Commission for Liturgy in 1986 and carried out by the Council for Research and Development. The reflections which follow are inspired by these needs, as are the proposals intended to meet them. The goal to be achieved is joyful, prayerful celebration and the proclamation of good news. These pages are aimed at helping pastors and people throughout Ireland achieve that goal.

This guide to the celebration of the word originated in a meeting of the Irish Commission for Liturgy in February 1986. It was decided there to carry out a survey of attitudes to preaching among people and clergy. It was also decided to go beyond social research and publish a statement on the celebration of the word in the light of this research. A sub-committee was set up consisting of Fr Brian Gogan CSSp, Faculty of Theology, Kimmage Manor, Fr Billy Fitzgerald, RTE, and Mr A.G. McGrady, Mater Dei Institute, Dublin. Subsequently, Dr Ann Breslin of the Council for Research and Development, Maynooth College, joined the group. Fr Peter Meldon of the Dublin Archdiocese assisted the committee for some time.

The sub-committee understood its task to be threefold: to

survey the attitudes of priests and people to the celebration of the word; to review the conclusions of this study in the context of current wisdom on the theology, celebration and proclamation of the word; to draw conclusions from these reflections which might improve the quality of ministry in the Sunday Eucharist. The findings of the 1986 survey resulted in three separate studies on the attitudes of adult laity, students and priests to the celebration of the word and preaching. These results were summarised by Dr Ann Breslin and her staff and form Part II of this book. (The full reports will be published separately by the Council for Research and Development.) A liturgical and theological study of the celebration of the word was prepared by Fr Brian Gogan, Fr Billy Fitzgerald and Mr Andrew G. McGrady. I have rewritten these reflections. They form the first of two parts. Part I is a guide to the celebration of the word; Part II is a summary of the research carried out by the Council for Research and Development.

Chapter 1 of Part I provides a short analysis of these research findings and examines the principal issues, problems and concerns they reveal. Chapter 2 reflects on the theology of the word and the light it sheds on its celebration and proclamation. This provides a firm theological basis for the celebration of the word. It may also pre-empt certain objections to the approach to preaching described later on. On the one hand preachers can use their own experience, the experience of others and of the world around them as a storehouse of examples to illustrate the message of tradition (the 'Fr Trendy syndrome'). On the other hand, those who criticise the use of everyday experience, anecdote, authentic human wisdom from whatever source, may dismiss this approach as mere 'gimmickry'. Chapter 2 shows how God's word comes to us in the world about us, within our own experience, as well as in the scriptures and the tradition of the Church. Divine revelation in its many forms can contribute to the effective proclamation of the word. Chapter 3 deals with more practical issues: who should be involved in the liturgical ministry of the word and how they should prepare for their task. It makes suggestions for effective celebration and the practice of preaching.

In editing this work I am indebted to Fr Anthony Geoghegan

CSSp and Fr Con Casey CSsR for comments on the theology of the word; to Fr Ivan Payne DCL for advice on canon law governing preaching; to Fr John Wall, Clonliffe College, for assistance with practical aspects of preaching; to Fr Pierce Murphy and Rev. Paul Hurley SVD for many practical suggestions concerning this text. I am grateful to the Irish bishops for funding this research, to Bishop Michael Harty and the members of the Irish Commission for Liturgy for their constant support and advice; most of all, I am indebted to the other members of the sub-committee who are, indeed, co-authors of this work.

Brian Gogan CSSp
Faculty of Theology
Holy Ghost Missionary College
Dublin 12

Part I

Channels of his word

*How today's gift and reception of
the divine word will influence
our celebration of the liturgy*

by
Brian Gogan CSSp

Chapter 1

To whom we preach

Audience research is a tool commonly used in the communications industry. Feedback mechanisms are built into most computerised systems. When the Church seeks the views and attitudes of the laity on some aspect of its mission, it does so with similar purposes in mind. It wants to find out how well it is doing in the eyes of the people. However, a deeper dimension also enters in. Consulting the laity, to adopt Newman's phrase, has another aspect to it. It is an attempt to discover what the Spirit of God is now saying in the hearts of his people in relation to the Church and its ministry. Such an enquiry may then lead to new developments in celebration and mission. These developments will, of course, be assisted by the practical assessments which people have offered.

Such considerations underlie the national survey of popular attitudes to the liturgy of the word, and to preaching in particular, carried out by the Council for Research and Development, Maynooth College, during 1986/87. This survey was addressed to two sections of the laity; adults and young people in their final year in post-primary school. Priests were also surveyed, both to discern what the Spirit is saying within them and to compare their views with those of the laity.

Systematic research is, of course, not the only way to carry out such enquiries and is a relatively new instrument for the discernment of spirits. Yet, the findings of the survey, when studied in the light of liturgical principle and a theology of preaching, suggest a special focus and a way forward for the celebration of the word in Ireland today. This report reviews these findings and explores the possibilities they indicate for the liturgical celebration of the word. Some of the figures cited in Part I are drawn from the full reports on attitudes to the liturgy of the word among priests, adult laity and students in Ireland, carried out by the Council for Research and Development in 1986. Hence, they may not be found in Part II of this book which is a summary of those reports.

The main impression created by the survey of lay attitudes to the present manner of celebration can be simply put. If the liturgy of the word is not in a state of crisis, it is definitely a problem area for all concerned with pastoral liturgy.

It may come as a surprise to some that most adults find all three Sunday readings helpful (72%, the first reading, 76%, the second reading, 92%, the gospel). The responsorial psalm has least impact, making a favourable impression on 58% of those questioned. The scripture lessons have less impact on students: 38% find the first reading in some way helpful, 40%, the second reading, 73%, the gospel, while the psalm gets a favourable reaction from only 28%. If most adults find the other readings of some help in their lives, most students get inspiration only from the gospel.

Liturgical readings do interest adults and students. Most adults find that they can listen to the readings (78%) and understand what they mean (74%). While little attempt is made to prepare the liturgy of the word or to reflect on the lessons after Mass, most adults and students will welcome some help in taking part in it. A large proportion of both adults (80%) and students (74%) want to understand its liturgical framework, while even more (89%, 74%) want good, brief introductions to the readings. Even more call for better readers (97%, 78%), while over half the students want the number of readings cut down (54%).

In short, while interest in the liturgical cycle of scripture does not go as far as personal study for most people, the majority of those who attend Sunday Mass want to understand better what is being read and benefit from it. While the positive response to the lessons read at Mass is encouraging, it also presents a challenge. There is a call here from the people to make the most of this opportunity to proclaim God's message, by helping them to understand the liturgical cycle of readings, by providing a context for the readings in short introductions, and by having the lessons read in a way which holds attention and conveys their meaning. Many who reflect on these responses will see the need to supplement liturgical guidance with adult education courses in scripture.

As with the readings, there is a marked, positive interest in the homily. Of those questioned in an earlier survey (1984) 84% wanted a homily at Mass. What kind of homily? Those asked in 1986/7 were quite explicit — a sermon which relates to life, starts one thinking, explains the message of the Gospel, does all this in simple terms, is brief and well-delivered.

As one might expect, most priests (92%) consider preaching an important part of their ministry. While some (26%) take a rather intellectual view of preaching — instruct, educate, explain, were the words they used to describe it — many (40%) agree with the laity. They see it as a link between life and scripture. They also agree that sermons should be simple, short and well-delivered. Hence, among laity and clergy there is a marked agreement on the importance of preaching and the style of homily required today.

On the other hand, most lay people (57%) are not satisfied with the quality of preaching now. More dissatisfied church-goers are found among the under-forties (79%), among single persons (68%), among those with second- and third-level education (67%, 73%), among city dwellers (67%). The majority of married people and country residents are also dissatisfied (54%, 57%). In short, the single, the city dwellers, the better-educated and, above all, the young (79%) do not feel the word of God is being well spoken to them in their Sunday celebration.

How do priests rate their own homilies? A similar, general question about how they felt they were getting their message across was not put to them. But when asked about the last sermon they had preached, most felt they had held people's attention (93%), made the readings relate to daily life (84%), provided guidelines for daily living (91%) and given an encouraging message (91%). If priests assess their standard of preaching as positively as this on a regular basis (not just on a single occasion), there is a major misunderstanding between them and their people on this score. It would take further research to establish this.

Does the survey suggest any reasons why many people do not find the homily helpful? Six main aspects of the problem were examined, each of which shed some light on the subject. These were: training and resources available to priests; selection of topics; preparation, presentation and delivery of sermons; assessment procedures; choice of speakers. The findings will be summarised under these headings.

Training and resources

As regards training in the preaching ministry, roughly half the priests (48%) felt their seminary training had been adequate. Many (40%) had attended post-ordination courses in communication, 80% found them helpful. A majority (57%) felt themselves adequately prepared for this ministry, but 64% expressed a wish for further training.

Most priests (67%) need more resources for their preaching ministry. These, they say, would be most conveniently located at a diocesan centre equipped with books, videos, periodicals and other sermon aid materials. It would also have video recording facilities, access to professional staff for advice on performance, as well as specialists to assist in theological, scriptural and spiritual matters. Replies to further questions suggest the need for a network of support centres reaching from parish, through deanery and diocesan to national level, with differing facilities available at each location. The lack of resources may undermine priests' best efforts.

Choice of topics

While priests sometimes have to tackle subjects not favoured by their congregations — sexuality, church finances, political issues, hell, Satan — the laity's list of preferred topics deserves attention.

The four highest preferences went to the life of Christ, family life, personal life and the Blessed Virgin. Students' preferences were even more life-centred than those of adults. They want their own particular problems addressed in the light of the Gospel. 'Talk about life and tell us how Scripture helps us to deal with it', seems to be the main emphasis in the laity's views on this matter. There is a notable difference between these preferences and those expressed by priests — the sacraments, God's love, prayer and justice. Some of these topics have an abstract, theological ring about them, not immediately directed to people's concerns. People's felt needs cannot determine the agenda for preaching. The preacher will have to be unpopular at times. Nonetheless, while presenting the word of God in all its fullness, the effective preacher will take stock of people's preferences and inclinations.

Composition and delivery

As regards composition and delivery of homilies both clergy and adult laity stressed the need for a clear message (86%, 94%). But while lay people favour storytelling, reference to the priest's own experience, and use of the congregation's experience, priests' preferences reverse this order. This suggests another area where people's expectations of the sermon are not met. A simple technique of gaining attention from the start may be missing from much preaching, as may be the use of examples which touch the imagination.

Laity and clergy agree that sermons should be brief. Clergy are less reluctant than laity to use creative techniques such as drama, mime or audio-visual equipment to support the sermon. A pattern of uncertainty on all sides emerges regarding this, due perhaps to lack of familiarity with their use. Most lay people agree that preachers should be brief and well-prepared, should speak clearly, keep to the subject and relate what they say to everyday life. Young people add, 'be interesting, bring in a touch of humour'. If too many of these qualities are missing, it will be difficult for the preacher to get his point home.

Homily preparation

When discussing success or failure in reaching the hearts of one's listeners with the word of God, the question of preparation must be looked at. Long-term preparation includes education, Christian life, witness and prayer. The questions raised in the survey focused more on short-term research, composition and rehearsal. Most priests (99%) agree that preparing sermons is an important part of their ministry. The majority (58%) of those who spend a *specific* length of time at the job (18% prepare 'throughout the week'), take two hours or less to organise their material and practise delivery of the Sunday sermon. Is this adequate? For some, perhaps. But it does not bear comparison with the level of rehearsal in the performing arts. Even an amateur theatre company will spend many hours in rehearsal apart from individual practice and with an already existing script. The preacher has to write his script and rehearse it. One of the keys to better sermons must lie in better preparation and that may mean more time.

Quite a number of priests spend a good deal of time preparing their sermons, consulting with other priests (42%) and laity (22%), reading the scriptures with the help of commentaries, referring to standard texts and periodicals which supply homily material. More than one priest in five spends three hours or more each week at this work. Perhaps these are the ones whose words reach their hearers and touch their hearts most deeply.

Professional communicators continually monitor their audiences in terms of the number of viewers, readers or listeners. Efforts are made to assess their satisfaction with the message received and to discover the direction of future trends in public taste. While such a sophisticated approach is hardly called for in the average parish, the simple question 'How am I doing?' could elicit a helpful response. In fact, less than one in ten of the lay people surveyed recall having their opinion asked about a recent sermon.

Assessment procedures

That being so, more than half the priests said they had asked a lay person's opinion of a recent sermon. If this is a regular practice, only a small range of people is being consulted. A more systematic and extended enquiry would help preachers target their words more accurately. In any event, if the homily is to shed light on the daily lives of the people, something more than ordinary pastoral contact may be required. Organised groups, where priests and people meet in assessing the previous week's homily and preparing the one to come, have been tried by some of the clergy (22%) and have been found helpful by almost all (90%) who have done so. Many of the laity, especially young people (53%), expressed an interest in helping with such preparation. As regards these groups, 68% had 3-12 members. Roughly half the groups were stable, the other half often changed membership. More than half had an equal mix of the sexes, while 42% were mainly made up of women. More than half had a membership under fifty years of age, and 42% a mixture of ages from eighteen upwards. The majority of members had at least post-primary education (88%). More than half the group had both married and single members, while a third had mainly married members. Priests working in cities were more likely to meet on a weekly basis than those in rural areas.

Choice of speakers

In a culture which provides multiple choices in many areas of life, one might assume that a change of preacher would prove helpful from time to time. This proposal meets with general approval among clergy and laity. In general, priests and people think it a good idea to bring in a visiting speaker, clerical, religious or lay. An occasional change of face and voice at the lectern keeps people's interest alive. A visiting priest is the most favoured choice (priests 93%, laity 90%, students 88%). Otherwise, priests and adult laity favour a lay person, religious brother or religious sister, in that order of preference. 81% of priests are open to lay interventions as compared with 72% of students and 66% of adult laity.

The main thrust of these comments suggests that the quality of preaching needs to be greatly stepped up. Against this it could be argued that those who are already committed to the Christian life in prayer, sacrament and service, draw fruit from Sunday preaching. These make up to a large extent the 43% who are satisfied. Hence, it could be said that the main need is to evangelise the other 57%, to change their hearts, so they will be ready to receive the word of God when preached to them on a week-to-week basis. This 57% are simply not attuned to the word of God. Until something fundamental happens in their lives, the preacher is wasting breath on desert air.

This argument has some foundation. Unless one has made a full commitment to Jesus Christ as Lord of one's life, accepted the inner guidance of the Spirit and the helps and duties of loyal membership of the Church, one will be deaf to the full message of revelation. Quite a number of those surveyed may not have made such commitment, remaining at a child's level of spiritual development, if not merely 'ritual' Catholics. How to deal with this very real problem lies outside the scope of this document.

On the other hand, the argument is not fully convincing. Most of those who find Sunday sermons unsatisfactory are interested in the word of God and its implications in their lives. 84% of those interviewed said they wished to hear a good homily on Sunday morning; 92% of adults and 73% of students find the gospel readings helpful. Allowing for the difficulty many people have in following a public reading and grasping its message at one sitting, this is a high percentage. Both sets of figures taken together indicate that the great majority of Sunday worshippers will take in a well-presented sermon, provided, of course, that their needs are met or their assumptions challenged. So, what is a good homily?

It would be a simple matter to draw up a list of 'do's and don't's' for preachers and a set of recommendations to competent authorities concerning the development of the liturgy of the word and the ministry of preaching. However, what is in question here is a process of discernment. Hence, the main issues and general directions that have emerged from the consultation of laity and clergy will be reviewed from the standpoint of scripture, tradition, liturgical principle and communications theory with a view to describing more accurately an approach to preaching which should prove effective. It may also deflect some preachers from two false views which can affect their preaching. One uses personal experience and the events of life as a bank of useful resource material to be used, as appropriate, in preaching. The other sees revelation as crystallised for all time in a set of statements in the Bible and in magisterial pronouncements. These views prevent the preacher contacting the deeper message addressed to preacher and people alike in nature, history and common experience, as well as in the ever-deepening understanding of scripture and tradition made possible by research.

Chapter 2

The word we proclaim

The crux of the problem in preaching seems to be the link between word and life. Most Mass-goers are enriched by the liturgical scripture lessons. There is a clear request from both adults and students for a better bridge between this word from God and their daily lives — in better homilies.

How to do this? This raises questions about the kind of homily given as well as its preparation, about who may preach, about resources used by the preacher in preparation and about the kind of topics chosen. It also raises the issue of one's understanding of divine revelation. What is the word of God being proclaimed and where is it to be found? If the word of God is preserved in a deep-freeze of doctrine, theology or scriptural text, then it is a simple matter to pass it on. One reads it, repeats it, explains it and applies it to concrete circumstances.

Before Vatican II many Catholic theologians and pastors looked on God's word somewhat in this way. Revelation is, they held, a fixed deposit of truths — safely preserved in a body of defined and accepted doctrines approved by the Church. The task of the religious teacher and preacher is to expound these doctrines and indicate a suitable response by the listener. This view of revelation together with pastoral needs has had a marked influence on the pattern of preaching in Ireland over the years.

Though not a great deal is known as yet about the tradition of preaching, evidence suggests that catechetical instruction has been one of its main concerns. In penal times and the period after it, this was understandable. In most cases the Sunday assembly was the priest's only opportunity of reaching his people. It may be safely concluded, writes Dr Patrick Corish, that '... Sunday preaching was essentially an extension of the catechism' (Corish, 210). If this was normal practice in the nineteenth century, it was sustained in living memory into recent times. Programmes of catechetical instruction listed topics for sermons at Sunday Mass within the accepted framework of religious instruction used in schools, based around the creed, commandments, sacraments and the Lord's prayer. These programmes provided a pre-selected topic with little connection with the readings of the day or the life of the community. The homilist expounded the familiar doctrine and preaching was largely divorced from the spiritual needs of the people. It also reflected a fixed 'doctrinal' understanding of the word of God. In its day this style of preaching met a serious pastoral need. It became less useful when education improved and people's needs grew more complex.

After Vatican II scriptural preaching came more into vogue. Unfortunately, a similarly 'fundamentalist' view of revelation has affected much biblical teaching. Once more God's word is seen by some to be firmly and immovably expressed in the literal sense of scripture. The task of the homilist is to explain the text provided in the liturgy of the day and indicate suitable responses. Some Dublin youngsters described this approach as 'more Scribes and Pharisees stuff!' That kind of remark hints at the underlying problem. Scribes and Pharisees don't walk the streets of Dublin in the same garb as in Jerusalem 2,000 years ago. Yet, Christ's warning about the pharisaical spirit applies as much today as then. The problem the homilist faces is how to find God's word in the scriptural phrase and make it live today. To do this he will have to find God's word alive in his own experience and interpret it by means of scriptural and other texts. But first he needs to understand how God speaks and where his word is to be found. Fortunately, Vatican II has given us a thorough exposition of the theology of the word, a theology which must underlie the celebration and ministry of the Gospel (DV passim, LG 9, GS 15, 44, NA 2-4, AG 9).

Vatican II makes it clear that God talks to us in many ways.

God speaks to Christians in their hearts. His word is present in creation. His word was present in a particularly powerful way in the history of the Jewish people. His word became completely one of us in the life and person of Jesus Christ. His word is reflected in the witness and teaching of his immediate followers, of their disciples and in the tradition of the Church.

With this background it becomes easier to build a bridge between God's word and life. God's word is already present in the life we are living. When we reflect on life we can understand it more clearly with the help of scripture, tradition, Church teaching and the insights of other believers. The apparent gulf between word and life is not 2,000 years of history and culture. It is the gap between event and understanding, fact and interpretation, obscurity and light.

In this document, we underline the pre-eminence of God's word. But we also point to the many ways in which this word comes to us. We show how each of these inflections of God's voice can enhance the celebration of the liturgy of the word and contribute to the composition and delivery of homilies. God's word understood in all its fullness is a vast storehouse from which the preacher can draw.

Before he can draw on this storehouse, he must know where it is and what it contains. A current understanding of revelation is the first step in defining what homily is and the many ways it may be given. The homilist proclaims the good news of Jesus Christ. But what is good news for this congregation, on this day, and where can it be found? That is the crux of the matter.

In the beginning was the word

An account of how God speaks to us must begin by quoting the opening chapter of John's Gospel.

> In the beginning was the Word, and the Word was with God, and the Word was God. He was in the beginning with God; all things were made through Him, and without Him was not anything made that was made .... and the Word became flesh and dwelt among us, full of grace and truth;

we have beheld his glory, glory as of the only Son from the Father. ... And from his fullness have we all received, grace upon grace ... (*Jn 1:1-3,14,16*)

To this we can add:

... that which we have seen and heard we proclaim also to you, so that you may have fellowship with us... (*1 Jn 1:3*)

In God self-knowledge and self-awareness develop into a word. This eternal Word (the Son), does not merely express all truth, it also speaks out awe and admiration at the divine mystery. It is the eternal spring of divine love, the source of the Spirit. Hence, the Christian God is three — not one — where the Father's self-awareness expressed in Word moves beyond insight and affirmation to the Spirit who is love. If our preaching is to move in the pathways of God, it must not end with imparting knowledge, but with promoting love, fellowship and community.

When our proclamation of the word begins with an experience of God, we come to know him and respond to him with awe, reverence and love. As we share this experience in our preaching, we go beyond teaching scripture, imparting doctrine and knowledge. We seek to evoke love, promote fellowship, build community — for this is how divine life manifests itself.

If we can share our knowledge of God in common speech, we will begin to meet the expectations of the laity for a preaching which relates to life, to their and our experience, and which is illustrated from contact with God. God is with them as well as with his ordained ministers. They seek words to describe and praise the one who comes to them. The preacher who knows the true God, as St Patrick did, will provide for the people, as Patrick did.

Christ with me, Christ before me, Christ behind me,
Christ in me, Christ beneath me, Christ above me,
Christ on my right, Christ on my left,
Christ when I lie down, Christ when I sit down,
Christ when I arise ...
I arise today.

Through a mighty strength, the invocation of the Trinity,
Through belief in the threeness,
Through confession of the oneness
Of the Creator of Creation.

(From *St Patrick's Breastplate*)

Of his fullness have we all received

For some, this encounter may be an experience as dramatic as that of Patrick, Paul or Augustine. For most, it will be the more or less steady awareness of God given in contact with others, with the world of nature and, most of all, in prayer and reflection on scripture. Jesus promised his disciples that he would make himself known to them and speak to them through his Spirit. When we are attuned to the presence of God, and aware of the blessing he brings to our lives, then we will want to share this news with others, as the Father expresses his awareness of himself in the divine mystery, and draws us into fellowship with himself. That is how the word was announced at Pentecost.

The Holy Spirit descended on the apostles. Of this event was born both a burning faith in Jesus Christ and a community marked by unity of mind and heart, shared possessions, common worship and dedication to apostolate.

God continues to reveal himself to those who believe in his name. He dwells in our hearts through his Spirit, enabling us to become citizens of the heavenly kingdom, brothers and sisters of Jesus Christ. This implies that the whole reality of God is somehow communicated in grace to each one. The grace of God, his very Spirit, imbues our being and sets our minds on a new course, reaching outwards in faith to the transcendent being of God. We may spend a lifetime trying to grapple with this mystery. Better, we may spend a lifetime abiding in it. It always goes before us, beyond reach of mind.

Yet it is also within. The mystery of God's presence dwells in us as in a temple. The God who dwells within is no idle God. He is the dynamic creator of the universe, the all-powerful ruler who guides the galaxies on their path, the humble redeemer tirelessly walking the land of Israel in search of lost sheep. This divine activity leaves its mark on our being. God's image is imprinted on our hearts like a footprint in sand. As the Letter to the Hebrews puts it, quoting the prophet Jeremiah, '...I will put my laws into their minds, and write them on their hearts, and I will be their God, and they shall be my people. And they shall not teach every one his fellow or every one his brother, saying, "Know the Lord", for all shall know me, from the least of them to the greatest' (*Heb 8:10-11*). The full reality of the divine Word is given to each one who enters the New Alliance.

The intimate, personal knowledge of God promised by Jeremiah has come as an overpowering gift to some of the saints. For most Christians it requires an active listening, a faith-filled awareness of God dwelling within them. This listening is usually best done with the written word of God at hand. The biblical word so often becomes the life-giving word by which God speaks to us within. The 'spiritual reading' of scripture in the monastic manner, biblical contemplation, for example in the Ignatian style, simple attention to God, are common ways used by Christians today to hear this word spoken in their hearts. Along with other means, these can enable the preacher to hear God's word spoken directly to him.

Whichever way we use, there is ample encouragement in the New Testament to leave ourselves open to God and to let him teach us directly about himself. This is one of the major themes of Jesus' final discourse at the last supper. 'And I will pray the Father, and he will give you another Counselor, to be with you for ever ... you know him, for he dwells with you, and will be in you' (*Jn 14:15-17*). This Counselor — whom we know, because he lives in us — will teach all things necessary for our salvation. 'But the Counselor, the Holy Spirit, whom the Father will send in my name, he will teach you all things, and bring to your remembrance all that I have said to you' (*Jn 14:25-26*).

The Spirit will teach us if we listen. What he teaches is what Christ taught by his life and words. What the Spirit does is guide us into the deeper meaning of Christ's revelation to his followers. The Spirit amplifies, interprets, applies the word Christ has given us, in our lives and the lives of our people. 'When the Spirit of truth comes, he will guide you into all the truth; for he will not speak on his own authority, but whatever he hears he will speak, ...he will take what is mine and declare it to you' (*Jn* 16:13-15).

If the Spirit teaches those commissioned for the ministry of the word, he also teaches other baptised Christians. The experience of God is not restricted to ordained clergy. The whole range of spiritual experience in Christian tradition is also at the preacher's disposal. More relevant to his real needs is the word God is speaking to the people around him — his fellow priests and parishioners.

Many of the laity — 53% of the young, 17% of the adults — say they are willing to help priests prepare their sermons. Such aid will take various forms. One important way the laity can help is by sharing with preachers their experience of the Lord. The God they meet may be the God of tempests, of joy, of calm, of light, the God of darkness, or of absence. Whichever face God shows may be the one this parish is waiting for. Open discussion between priest and people will make it possible for the preacher to present this word from God to a wider audience.

In practice, much of this sharing will take place informally as people chat or talk in casual meetings, pastoral visits, Christian action, prayer or study groups of various kinds. There may also be a need to have formal groups for sermon preparation. Though few Irish priests (22%) use such groups, those who do, have found them beneficial (90%). Homily preparation groups could well be an important way of finding God's word in life today, of hearing the word he speaks in people's hearts, of knowing his message to this parish at this time.

Whether the Blessed Virgin appeared at Knock may be a matter for debate. What seems most likely, in faith, is that God spoke a word to the people concerned. The message was heard and conveyed to a wider audience. It continues to echo in our own time. God still speaks to his people as to his priests. This is one of the main resources the preacher has for his homily. When preparing for the Sunday liturgy, the preacher will receive both inspiration and apt illustration, sometimes even the words themselves, if he reflects both on his own human and spiritual experience and that of his parishioners. Such listening may lead to a word as powerful in its own way as the message of Knock.

Nothing was made without him

Life is not limited to our immediate contact with God, nor is God's revelation of himself limited to the word he speaks in our hearts. Human life itself and the environment in which it is lived are the work of God's hands. The tragedies and successes of daily life in the cycle of birth, growth, career, marriage, family, sickness and death — all are shaped by the divine hand. The blueprint is the eternal Word of God. If this is true of personal life, it is equally true of the course of history itself (Acts 17:26-27).

This is crystal clear in the Bible. Beginning with Abraham and running through the saga of his descendants, through the Mosaic and Davidic cycles, the chronicles of kingdom and exile, there is an explicit awareness of the intervention of God in the life of his people. The Bible itself also testifies that God's providence controls the whole of human history. God's plan is working out not merely in the Judaeo-Christian tradition but in the lives of all peoples. The events of world history — as of those of our local community — are part of the unfolding plan of God for the human race. They contain within them a hidden word of God — of encouragement, of judgement, of challenge or reproach, an invitation to rejoice or to hope against hope. Parishioners meet this history in daily life. They have to cope with its crises, weather its storms, submit to its mystery, retain hope in the face of its tragedies.

In Ireland, today, issues demand our attention — family problems, unemployment, the Northern troubles, violence and crime, emigration — we all have our own private list. If the preacher is to address life's problems he will have to deal with these issues and in doing so he may have to say unpopular things. The laity listed among topics they want to hear least about: politics (adults 25%), sex (adults 9%, students 13%), drug and alcohol abuse (students 11%). Both sexuality and politics in the broad sense enter into most areas of social tension. They will not be avoided but the preacher will tread warily knowing how sensitive these issues are.

From another point of view it is important that homilists deal with the main issues of the day. The triumphs and tragedies of the community, local and worldwide, are what educators call 'teachable moments' when public interest is aroused and attention easily held. We feel this most profoundly in moments of family celebration or mourning. The same applies to the community. A young person is killed in a car crash, a group of young people volunteer for Ethiopian famine relief, TV pictures show thousands caught in floods in Sudan, an atomic power plant leaks its effluent into the atmosphere. The word and hand of God are involved in these events. Christians have to react to them, perhaps take an active part in opposing them or in carrying them further. These are times when a well-briefed preacher will be listened to. That briefing presupposes a well-stocked library, an educated awareness of current affairs and a willingness to consult with well-informed colleagues.

The true light that enlightens everyone

In conflict situations it is not always easy to discern the divine word shaping our lives. When we examine the religious history of the world, study the writings of eastern mystics, or meet followers of other world religions and philosophies, it is easier to see God's grace at work '...from his fullness have we all received'. The average pastor may not be over-keen on perusing the Koran or studying the writings of Confucius. Yet in a world which has, for many, become 'a global village', allusions to the wisdom of other traditions may prove helpful. Western people today may be too impressed with the flight from God they see going on around them. It can be useful to recall that the West is a declining percentage of the world's population. Many millions of people worship God devoutly in the Muslim, Hindu, Buddhist and animist traditions. Their life experience, religious writing and practice may also shed light on doubting or questioning hearts in an Irish college, school, youth group or professional association, as can the life experience and practice of sincere agnostics. Rich gems of wisdom are to be found in the writings of ancient times, as well as in those of moderns like Gandhi and Tagore, Martin Buber, Anne Frank, Sakharov and Roger Garaudy, to name a few.

Beginning with St Paul in the Areopagus (*Acts 17:28*), the

Church has made use of 'pagan wisdom' and philosophy to interpret revelation and to unravel its apparent contradictions. Today, equally well, non-Christian writers can be the vehicle of divine wisdom. Apt quotation can help the word of God preached in a Sunday assembly where listeners are aware that there is more than one way of looking at reality. Striking quotes from non-Christian sources can support positions common to believers and true humanists.

The groups least satisfied with the Sunday homily are precisely those most sensitive to pluralism — the under-forties (79%), second- and third-level graduates (67%, 73%). In allowing diversity of opinion one respects their vision of the world. In using the insights of other traditions one brings God's word to them in a language they may listen to with interest. As, for example, on violence, Gandhi's remark has weight: 'Conquer hatred with love, falsehood with truth, violence with patient suffering'. Christ's teaching of course too — but surely relevant to Ireland's present concerns.

In him all things were made

Few of the world's great teachers used the imagery of nature to better effect than Jesus himself. The example of the birds in the air and the lilies of the field, the parable of the sower, the allegory of the vine have re-echoed down the ages. The power of these images is great not merely because they are apt but because they reveal in themselves the purpose and providence of God. 'In the beginning was the Word ... all things were made through him ...' (Jn 1:1-3). The divine Word has left his imprint in nature, in its stones and clouds and plants. The world about us reveals God to us, his presence, his plan, his providence.

This sense of the world of nature as God's handiwork inspired many of the finest psalms. 'By the word of the Lord the heavens were made, and all their host by the breath of his mouth. He gathered the waters of the sea as in a bottle; he put the deeps in storehouses' (Ps 33:6-7). The elements not merely reflect the artistry of God, they are his mouthpiece. 'The voice of the Lord is upon the waters; the God of glory thunders, the Lord, upon many waters. The voice of the Lord is powerful, the voice of the Lord is full of majesty' (*Ps 29:3-4*).

An Indian sage put it a little strongly when he said, 'There is nothing in the world that is not God'. The English poet Elizabeth Browning struck a more familiar note; 'Earth is crammed with heaven and every common bush afire with God, but only those who see take off their shoes. The rest will sit around and pick blackberries'. That sense of the presence and power of God in nature is a steady current in Celtic tradition from pre-Christian times to the work of poets like Ó Direáin, Kavanagh and Heaney. The flow's source is suggested by verses ascribed to Amergin in the *Leabhar Gabhála*: 'I am a salmon in the water, I am a lake in the plain, I am a word of science, I am the point of the lance of battle, I am the God who created in the head the fire. Who is it who throws light into the meeting on the mountain? Who announces the ages of the moon? Who teaches the place where couches the sun?' Pre-Christian Ireland had already perceived some of what St Patrick said, in lines ascribed to him: 'I arise today — through the strength of heaven: Light of sun, Radiance of moon, Splendour of fire, Speed of lightning, Swiftness of wind, Depth of sea, Stability of earth, Firmness of rock'.

Nature is not merely a helpful resource for homely or striking images. It is a place where God can be met, heard, spoken to and adored. In such encounters with God in nature we will find the word to meet the needs of troubled hearts, to calm the impatient spirit, to encourage the downhearted, to give reason to the joyful to celebrate. Nature imagery will be most effectively used with congregations who themselves are steeped in nature. Perhaps all they do is 'pick blackberries'. A preacher who finds God in 'the wind which breathes upon the sea' or in 'the murmur of the billows' will help the blackberry pickers find something more in the bush from which they collect the fruit. Sadly, those who live in the concrete jungle will find it hard to share this experience of the transcendence and intimate presence of God.

He came to his own home

An encouraging and, perhaps, surprising aspect of the *Survey on the Liturgy of the Word* was adult reaction to the Old Testament — 72% found some help in the liturgical readings from the early part of the Bible. The Old Testament has not played a great role in Catholic religious education in Ireland. Unlike the Protestant churches, preaching based on the histories and prophecies of the ancient alliance has not been a common style of instruction. The response of the people to these readings indicates that the Spirit is indeed speaking to the people of our time through the experience of those who waited in fidelity to the Old Law for the coming of the Saviour.

We are well aware that these sacred books are the word of God. As the Second Letter to Timothy puts it 'All scripture is inspired by God and profitable for teaching...' (*3:16*), and the writer adds '... that the man of God may be complete, equipped for every good work' (*3:17*). The man who said 'Reading the Old Testament was like reading yesterday's newspaper today' was wrong. We need to know the histories, prophecies and poems of the Old Alliance, if, as the letter to Timothy puts it, 'we are to...be complete, equipped for every good work'.

Jesus himself was nourished on the Old Testament. From his earliest years he must have listened to the passages read weekly in the synagogue, perhaps memorised them with the facility of people where books are scarce. Luke shows him in the Temple, '... sitting among the teachers, listening to them and asking them questions' (*Lk 2:46*). Those who heard him were amazed at his understanding and his answers. Luke is saying that the Law and the Prophets were food and drink to Jesus — not merely chapter and verse but the inner meaning of the revelation of God's saving action in the history and wisdom of his chosen people. The synagogue must have been a familiar place to him. Jesus began his own ministry of the word, according to Luke 4:14-30, in his home place, preaching on Isaiah 61:1-2. Many of his other sermons were given, according to the evangelists, during the synagogue liturgy of the word, notably the discourse on the bread of life in John 6.

God's word comes to us clearly through the Old Testament

and can be used, as our Protestant brethren do so often effectively, as a basis for preaching. The great epics of the ancient history — the Abraham cycle, the Mosaic and Davidic cycles, the chronicles of divided kingdom, exile and return all reveal God's providence, his judgement and his mercy towards his people. All reveal patterns of human life with which we are familiar and can shed light on our own experiences of epiphany, darkness, disobedience, conversion, forgiveness, exodus and return. In all of them God is present with his saving love as in the epic events of his chosen people.

God's word speaks not merely through events but also in the poetry, the prophetic and wisdom literature of the Old Alliance. God's covenant word expressed his unfailing promise to his people and leads naturally to the covenant ratified anew in each celebration of the Eucharistic sacrifice. In many places the prophetic word rings out today as loudly as in the days of Jeremiah and Isaiah. The call to justice, wholeness and freedom from the clarion voices of Eastern Europe and Latin America, whether it be Lech Walesa or Archbishop Romero, as well as from voices in our own community, is an echo of the prophetic messages of the Old Testament.

The ancient wisdom books are full of homely advice on family, friendship, love and business. Ecclesiastes' poem on the transience of life (1:2-11) the picture of the good wife (*Prov 31:10-31*), the joyful description of human love in the Song of Songs can illuminate our present-day experience, can help identify and explain the puzzles which confront us in our daily struggle. Sadly, the Psalter, that great book of Christian prayer, made least impression on the laity (58%). Perhaps psalms must be sung and not recited, if their more subtle flavour is to be tasted.

The word was made flesh

The gospel of Jesus Christ complements the divine indwelling in our hearts as the clearest way God speaks to us. If the Spirit of God comes to us through grace, we need the Word of God and the written record of his sayings and doings in the flesh to interpret the urgings of the Spirit. As John puts it, Jesus is 'the true light that enlightens every man ... coming into the world' (*Jn 1:9*). The life of Jesus, the light of the world, shines into every heart, illumines every situation, helps overcome every defeat, and points the way to final victory. The gospels are certainly the main source the homilist will use to let God's word guide his listeners on life's journey.

Jesus is the Word made flesh, like to us in all things save sin. His human experience and his words of wisdom can help most people with their problems. Take some of the negative aspects of his life: he has shared the fate of those conceived outside marriage, the socially marginalised, the colonised, those rejected by loved ones, betrayed by friends, condemned by society, bruised and broken in body, unjustly condemned, tortured, those in despair or in spiritual darkness, the dying and the dead.

One could similarly list Jesus' share in the joyful mysteries of human existence. Look at his role as liberator of the oppressed, protector of the innocent and, above all, as model of a loving, confident, childlike relationship to a heavenly Father. As the letter to the Hebrews so tersely says: 'In many and various ways God spoke of old to our fathers by the prophets; but in these last days he has spoken to us by a Son, whom he appointed heir of all things...' (*1:1-2*). Jesus is the last word from God about himself, the world, the human condition and its final salvation.

The universal appeal of Jesus even at a time when many seem to turn away from God is one of the more heartening aspects of our age. This appeal is seen in the interest shown by Irish adults and teenagers in the gospel read at Sunday Mass. Most find it helpful (adults 92%, students 73%). This is a solid base for the homilist to build on. Indeed, most priests (96%) make frequent use of the gospel reading in their sermons. In this way they are in tune with their congregation and can hardly fail to strike the right note.

Apart from the gospels, many of the other passages in the New Testament might well seem somewhat complex for the average churchgoer. Yet, most adults (76%) are helped by the apostolic writings used in the liturgy, though only a minority of students (40%) appreciate their use. This may explain why only a few priests (13%) often refer to the second reading in their homilies.

Another reason of course, is the fact that the main theme for celebration in the Sunday Eucharist is shared between Old Testament and gospel lessons.

Still, there is a rich vein of gold to be exploited in the apostolic writings. 'The Word of God, which is the power of God for salvation to everyone who has faith (cf. Rom 1:16), is set forth and displays its power in a most wonderful way in the writings of the New Testament' (*DV* 17). If the gospel has the place of honour in the scriptures, the writings of the apostles are also the word of God and carry that 'power of God for salvation'. Some of the more obscure chapters of St Paul might take more than a five-minute homily to explain. Yet, there are many splendid passages in the epistles to enrich the Sunday homily.

The apostles themselves felt the need to find other words and images, to develop and expound the central tradition they had received from Christ. Paul, in particular, claims a special revelation for himself to enrich his preaching. The need for variety, the search for fresh examples, for new angles on the topic of the day is an age-old problem for every teacher. The development of Jesus' message by the apostolic Church can be as helpful to people today as in the first century AD. Paul's great themes of justification by faith, freedom in the Spirit, John's teaching on the primacy of love, the apocalyptic imagery of the last times express in fresh language the teaching of Jesus. Indeed, to hear the New Testament message in all its richness we need the words of the apostles.

How the preacher fits this into his programme will be for him to decide. The three-year cycle of the Sunday Lectionary might well be a framework for stressing the apostolic teaching. Having based his preaching on the gospels for one cycle, the preacher might move to the apostolic writings for another.

God still speaks

If public revelation closed with Christ and the apostolic writings, the Christian community still passes on his word. Over the centuries God has spoken to his people, and through his Spirit has communicated himself to their hearts. The written record of revelation and the guidance of pastors have enabled them to understand, expand and apply this word of God to their own situation and time. The same work goes on today. The writings of saints, mystics, theologians, scholars, artists and poets of every century, but particularly our own, re-echo the word of God for us. This is a vast resource on which the homilist can draw for insight in the task of handing on the word. At the same time the Spirit-guided teaching of councils, popes and bishops provides him with sound answers to the challenges and disputed questions of the day.

The word of God comes to us in many ways. The role of the preacher is to mediate, speak the word not merely as it was *heard* in the past but as it is being *spoken* here and now in the minds and hearts of his people. This is one major response by the people to the *Survey on the Liturgy of the Word*. They want the homilist to address life today with its challenges, victories, defeats, doubts, and questions. To do this is not to abandon revelation, ignore doctrine, betray tradition. It is, rather, truly to hear God revealing himself today; it is to discuss those aspects of doctrine people will listen to today; it is to hand on tradition as an answer to people's problems today. God's word today is *kairos*, the moment of salvation. It must not be missed.

This is no easy task. The preacher is asked to share the word in its widest implications as well as in its immediate concrete application. He must draw on all the resources at his disposal; read the signs of the times; understand the movement of the Spirit in his own life; listen to the word spoken in the hearts of the faithful; expound the written word of scripture, especially the gospels; see the deeper currents of tradition reflected in the wisdom of the ages, the writings of the fathers and of contemporary theologians, wise people and prophets. In the light of all this, the preacher's role is to mediate to people of this day the transcendent Word of God. The preacher's ability to do this will determine to a large degree how well his people will be able to discern both the presence and absence of God, recognise the face of both good and evil in the world.

For evil and sin, God's word is one of judgement. Denunciation of what is untrue, unjust, unloving in human relationships, institutions and the practices of those who control them is part of the homilist's task. He will, naturally, remember the Saviour's example and love the sinner while hating the sin. Annunciation is his happier role, pointing to the active presence of God even in the obscure issues of our times. Annunciation leads easily to praise, to repeat Mary's Magnificat, to Eucharist.

In this context, the liturgy of the word, and the homily in particular, must be seen as part of God's self-revelation of his inner being. This began when God made the world and reached its highest point in the death and resurrection of Jesus. Christ is always present in his Church, especially in her liturgical celebrations. He is present in the Mass in the person of his minister. He is present in his word since it is he himself who speaks when the scriptures are read in Church. He is present and active in the preaching of his word (*SC* 7, *DVD* 24).

Chapter 3

The celebration of the word

1
The liturgy of the word

The gift of God's word is an intrinsic part of his saving action in the world, an essential part of the saving mystery which surrounds our life and which we celebrate in liturgy. God's word wells up within us through the urging of the Spirit. It reaches us from without in the events of the world about us, in the words of people of good will of every age, in the elements of nature, and above all in the scriptures. Because it is part of the saving mystery, a saving event in its own right, the word of God rightly forms an essential part of the celebration of the mystery of salvation.

Indeed, it can be said that every liturgical celebration is both a commemoration and proclamation of God's gift of revelation. Every liturgical celebration has at its centre the Paschal Mystery of Christ. In this Mystery is revealed the over-arching plan of God's dealing with the world. Jesus in his Paschal Mystery is the supreme revelation of God; who he is for us and how he wants us to respond to him. Every time we meet in liturgy to praise, worship and recall in rite this mystery of redemption we are celebrating the saving word of God, the eternal Word of God made flesh in the life story of Jesus Christ.

On the other hand, God's word is proclaimed in and through the entire liturgical action. As one writer puts it, 'Everything in liturgy preaches.' The *Liturgical Constitution* expresses this well when it says: '... the prayers addressed to God by the priest who, in the person of Christ, presides over the assembly, are said in the name of the entire holy people and of all present. And the visible signs which the sacred liturgy uses to signify invisible divine things have been chosen by Christ or by the Church. Thus not only when things are read "which were written for our instruction" (*Rom 15:4*), but also when the Church prays or sings or acts, the faith of those taking part is nourished, and their minds are raised to God so that they may offer him their spiritual homage and receive his grace more abundantly' (*SC* 33).

The thanksgiving prayer of the Eucharist is itself a proclamation of the Lord's death and resurrection till he comes. But the whole ritual by which we worship declares the wonderful deeds of God, affirms his loving kindness towards us and impels us to share this love with others. Hence, everything in the celebration of the entire liturgy must be so arranged and executed as to bring about the full, active participation of all those present (*SC* 14).

If a preacher gives a fine homily but follows on with careless celebration of the Eucharist, something is wrong. Were the preacher's faith fully informed it would inevitably express itself in reverent ritual, well-chosen music and song, and a style of worship involving the whole congregation. Speech alone does not convey the word of God at any time, least of all in liturgical assembly. Ritual, symbol, music, movement, prayer and silence combine to bring the word home to those who, with living faith, take part. If one's best efforts at preaching apparently fail, one can take comfort in this. God's word works powerfully through liturgy that is joyfully and prayerfully celebrated.

That being so, if only to scotch once and for all the ancient Irish heresy that 'real Mass begins at the three bells', we review the main reasons for including a celebration of the word in each liturgical service. The Eucharist was originally celebrated in the context of a Christian fellowship without formal preparation in the liturgy of the word. However, the Church decided early on that the best preparation for the Eucharist was a celebration of the word based, in all probability, on the synagogue service. Vatican II made it quite clear that it is essential that every sacramental celebration of the mystery of Christ should include the proclamation of and prayerful reflection on his saving word in scripture and in the Church.

Faith is remembered

If we celebrate the word because of its intrinsic role in the mystery of salvation, there are even more immediate reasons for including it in the Eucharistic liturgy. Every sacrament is a *sacrament of faith*. This is true in the fullest sense of the word in the acclamation after the consecration: 'Let us proclaim the mystery of faith'. In this we affirm our faith in Christ, the Saviour. We also affirm that this whole celebration is a proclamation of the faith of the Church. If it is to be a proclamation in living faith, this faith needs to be stirred up, the seed needs to be watered. The liturgy of the word is not merely a celebration of a saving event, it is almost an essential preparation for the celebration of the Eucharist. The word is proclaimed, reflected on, expounded and prayed over so that faith will be renewed and this celebration of Eucharist will be truly a celebration of faith. If this is done, the mystery of faith will be proclaimed authentically in the sacramental rite.

Jesus is remembered

Another reason for celebrating the word arises from a primary significance of Eucharist commanded by Christ: 'Do this... in remembrance of me' (*1 Cor 11:24-26*). In each Eucharist we remember the mystery of Christ. The liturgical texts focus on the principal aspects of that mystery. For example, in the offering prayer following the words of the proclamation of faith, we remember on various occasions the birth, death, resurrection, ascension and second coming of the Saviour. We do this each time we celebrate Eucharist. However, we also remember, for example in the preface, other aspects of the mystery of Christ appropriate to a particular day. Remembering forms an intrinsic

45

part of the celebration of the Eucharist and this is carried on in a powerful way in the celebration of the word. There we fix on specific words of the Lord, on specific events of his life, we listen once more to specific teachings of the apostles or accounts of spectacular interventions of God in the history of Israel. We put these forward to the faithful as distinctive points of remembrance, or as motives for thanksgiving in this particular celebration.

We all have many commemorations during our lives. We remember significant events on certain occasions — the days of birth, marriage, ordination, graduation, getting or leaving a job, springtime and harvest, and so forth. So too when we remember Christ we do not merely remember him in his central mystery of Passover and Exodus but also in the detail of his life on earth. And we give thanks.

We remember covenant

A third reason for celebrating the word also springs from the inner nature of Eucharistic celebration. The Eucharist commemorates the *covenant sacrifice* of Christ and makes it present. Every Eucharist involves renewal of the covenant making present the blood poured out to seal that agreement. It is received inwardly as a sign of our adherence to that alliance. But the covenant embraces in all its fullness, more than God's pledge of the indwelling Spirit, and on our side the commitment to follow the law of love. It also involves full fidelity to the whole word of God, to the whole of revelation and to all its demands. Hence, as we celebrate covenant sacrifice in the Eucharist, we recall, as did the leaders of the Old Testament, some of the terms of this covenant. We do so in the scripture readings and their explanation in homily before we proceed to a public and communal reaffirmation of our commitment to the covenant in the Eucharist (cf. Jos 24, Dt 27:1-9; 2 Kings 23:1-3 et al; Ne 8-9).

We break bread ...

Other reasons can be found too for the celebration of the word and linking it with the Eucharist. St John has told us in chapter 6 of his Gospel that the living bread, the living word we receive in faith, is also the bread we receive in the sacrament. That underlying unity is affirmed and reinforced each time we celebrate the word before celebrating Eucharist. As the introduction to the Missal puts it: 'In the Mass both the table of God's word and the table of Christ's body are prepared, so that from them the faithful may be instructed and nourished' (*IGMR* 8). And it adds '... When the sacred scriptures are read in church, God himself is speaking to his people, and Christ, present in his word, is proclaiming his Gospel. Hence the readings from God's word are among the most important elements in the liturgy and all who are present should listen to them with reverence' (*IGMR* 9).

The discussion of the ways in which God's word comes to us drew attention to the privileged function of the New and Old Testament writings in the transmission of the divine message. Naturally, these have the most honoured place in the liturgy of the word, just as the inspired prayer of the psalmist leads our response. But other expressions of God's word also have their place in the liturgy. The central tradition of the Church enshrined in the creed is both proclamation and response on Sundays and solemnities. In the prayer of the faithful we respond with our petitions, not merely to the word proclaimed in the assembly, but also to the word which touches our hearts and our daily lives.

The homily, par excellence, is the place where God's voice, heard in many ways, offers a simple message, which is God's word today. Jesus is the model for this in the sermon he preached in the Nazareth synagogue. Having read Is 61:1-2, '... he closed the book.... and he began to say to them, "Today this scripture has been fulfilled in your hearing" ' (*Lk 4:16-21*).

2

Ministers of the Word

In its teaching, life and worship, the Church maintains intact and transmits to each generation all that it is, all that it believes, so that over the centuries it may never cease to advance towards the fullness of divine truth (*DVD* 8). Most of the work of transmitting revelation is carried on by the people of God themselves, the laity. This takes place in the ordinary circumstances of family life and social living as well as through the activities of religious educators, teachers and catechists. Individual Christians receive special help (or charisms) from the Holy Spirit to enable them to continue on the task of teaching, prophesying and evangelising in a ministry carried out under the guidance of the pastors of the Church (1 Cor 12: 3-11; 27-29; Eph 4: 11-12; *LG* 7, *AG* 28).

By reason of their mission, the college of bishops, in communion with the Supreme Pontiff, and each bishop in his own local Church, are constituted true and authentic teachers of the faith. The bishop's responsibility is twofold. He preaches the gospel himself. He oversees the task of handing on the faith by those whom he appoints and by those who do so by virtue of their baptismal consecration (*CD* 2, 12-15).

The principal co-operators of the bishops in the ministry of the word are ordained priests and deacons. '... in virtue of the sacrament of Orders, after the image of Christ, the supreme and eternal priest (Heb 5: 1-10; 7:24, 9:11-28), they are consecrated in order to preach the Gospel and shepherd the faithful as well as to celebrate divine worship as true priests of the New Testament' (*LG* 28). Vatican II's decree on the priesthood sees the ministry of the word as the primary duty of ordained priests: '... it is the first task of priests as co-workers of the bishops, to preach the Gospel of God to all men. In this way they carry out the Lord's command; "Go into all the world and preach the Gospel to every creature" (*Mk 16:15*) and thus set up and increase the People of God' (*PO* 4).

Within the liturgical assembly the task of proclaiming and expounding the word is conferred on those who 'by ordination have been given the office of teaching and to those to whom the exercise of the ministry has been assigned', that is ordained ministers and other members of God's people authorised to proclaim and share the word (*DVD* 8).

There will be a welcome for lay people who 'proclaim and share the word' in the course of the liturgy. Among the clergy, more than 80% approve of talks given by laity, religious sisters and brothers. Among laity themselves, more than 60% of adults and 70% of students support this suggestion. Such intervention can both enrich and add variety to the ministry of the word. Pope Paul VI in *Evangelii Nuntiandi* sets a genuinely open and encouraging headline in a passage that is worth quoting in full: 'It is with the greatest joy that we see a multitude of pastors, religious and laymen who, in their zeal for the task of preaching Christ, are seeking constantly to improve the proclamation of the gospel. We fully approve the open approach which the Church of our time has adopted in pursuance of this objective. There is an openness to ... ecclesial ministries capable of renewing and strengthening the vigour of our evangelization' (*EN* 73).

The Irish Episcopal Conference has made provision for laity to share in the proclamation of the word at Mass, in its *Decrees*. 'In accordance with the prescription of Can. 766, the Irish Episcopal Conference, while stressing that the homily at any Mass may be given only by a priest or deacon (cf. *Can. 787:1*), hereby decrees that in the circumstances of this country it may in some particular cases be advantageous (though rarely, if ever, necessary) to allow a lay person to preach in a church or oratory, provided permission is given by the diocesan Bishop, even by way of general regulation' (*The Decrees of the Irish Episcopal Conference*, 7). The official commentary spells this out further. 'It is obviously not possible to detail all the situations in which this could arise, the more so since the *Decree* speaks not of general situations but rather of "particular cases": so much will depend upon the actual circumstances, not only in each diocese but perhaps even in each parish. One can, however, think of a number of subject matters where it might well be considered appropriate and helpful: thus, for example, the apostolate of charity to the poor and the suffering, the apostolate of prayer, the apostolate of the family, vocations, justice, and so on in regard to many spheres of the Church's life in which the laity are actively and essentially engaged. It may indeed sometimes happen that preaching by a lay person on one of these topics would be associated with an appeal for funds, but it must be borne in mind that, since this is a question of "preaching", the thrust must always be in the context of the Church's mission. Consequently, those to whom such permission is given must be experienced and well-prepared.'

Whoever preaches God's word, cleric, religious or lay Christian, must be well prepared for the task. Preparation begins with a life style which is geared for this ministry. The witness of a life of discipleship, lived by Gospel values, is the foundation stone of all preaching. In the last resort inner sincerity of heart is the main sounding board the Spirit uses to pronounce God's word. St Paul put this forcefully to the Corinthians when he wrote, 'If I speak in the tongues of men and of angels, but have not love, I am a noisy gong or a clanging cymbal' (*1 Cor 13:1*). The stumbling words of a saintly preacher will convey God's message better than the greatest eloquence of a sham disciple. The preacher's life is the strongest word he can utter.

A life of union with God will naturally express itself in prayer. Such prayer is part of the preparation for preaching. Prayerful listening to the word of God in scripture, meditation on the life of Jesus, attentive celebration of the liturgy of the hours, faithful reception of the sacraments (*PO* 18) as well as active, pastoral service to the people (*PO* 13) will keep the preacher in the presence of God. He will be ready to hear the word God wants him to share with his people.

God's word comes to the preacher through the lives of the people among whom he lives as well as in his own heart. In order to hear this word he will listen to, as well as speak with the people. Listening is not primarily a special function one carries out. It is, rather, openness to the Lord's voice in the daily lives of his parishioners. At the same time, many priests have found it helpful to do this in a systematic way — 20% have tried this, 90% found it helpful.

While spiritual reading of scripture is of paramount importance in listening for God's word, it should be matched by a correct understanding of the text. The preacher may not be a fully trained exegete but he can make use of the many tools at his disposal to discover the original meaning of the word proclaimed in scripture. Fundamentalism and fanciful interpretations of the word of God are twin evils to be avoided. With this in mind, a preacher will have a basic library of reference books such as standard commentaries, gospel parallels, biblical and theological dictionaries, as well as current reviews. With these he will avoid the excesses of a piety without solid foundation in the revealed word of God. Among the most popular sources for such study among Irish priests at present are *Scripture in Church* (used by 29%), Kevin O'Sullivan, *Sunday Readings* (Chicago 1970, 1971, 1972) (10%), William Barclay, *Daily Study Bible* series (Edinburgh, 1976) (8%). If biblical research went a little deeper, it might bring even better results.

However, the homilist's role is not merely to expound the scriptures as they were written. It is to link that word with the life of people today. To do this, study of tradition in the teaching of the Church and the writings of theologians is another way to hear God's word on another frequency. Theologians and the *magisterium* are already working in a more general, systematic way on this problem. They may provide the insights sought by the preacher to answer a particular question, deal with a special problem, identify a troublesome issue, challenge a prevailing fashion. More ready-made solutions are found in a variety of homiletic aids. Among the more popular with Irish priests are Flor McCarthy, *Sunday and Holyday Liturgies* (Dublin, 1984) (used by 23% of priests), *The Furrow* (22%), *Intercom* (20%), *The Living*

Word (11%). Such pre-packaged material and other publications on the market are useful resources but, of course, they are no substitute for the homilist's own personal experience, research, reflection or consultation with fellow priests and parishioners in preparing his Sunday talk.

The people who come to church on Sunday live in a certain society and culture. To understand people, and the various pressures they are under, one needs to grasp the undercurrents of feeling, value, movement, convention, taboo and expectation of this society and culture. While all this can be studied in a scientific way, if one keeps in touch with a society's art through literature, drama, radio, TV and cinema as well as the plastic arts, one can get a 'feel' for what is really happening. Who revealed the falsehoods of early twentieth century Ireland better than Pádraig Pearse? Who pricked the bubble of an abstract nationalism better than Sean O'Casey? Artists can often be prophets of the times. They uncover the deeper trends in culture, observe the shifting values, identify the spiritual crisis of an epoch, as did Eliot's *Wasteland*. In listening to them, one may begin to read the signs of the times, see where the Spirit of God is truly moving or where he is calling for specific reaction.

The people of God are not merely living in a certain culture, they are bound to a particular socio-economic and political system. Again, this is the work partly of God's hands, partly of human sinfulness. To understand it and assess it, to see God's word in it, is the preacher's task. To do this he will keep in touch with daily events, but he needs to do more than scan the headlines. He will follow more detailed commentary on the contemporary scene through the better columnists in the weekly press, the more analytical programmes on radio and TV, as well as Church reviews such as *Intercom, The Furrow, Doctrine and Life, America* and *The Tablet* and their secular counterparts.

The fact that only 7% of priests reported reading the newspapers as part of their homily preparation does not mean they are out of touch with current affairs and the deeper trends of the times. But it could mean that many do not see it as part of their job as preachers to comment. Yet, if Archbishop Desmond Tutu were silent on racism, if Bishop Helder Camara had remained quiet about the plight of Recife's poor, if Pope John Paul II failed to speak out on the destruction of family life in the western world, how much poorer this world would be! Not every preacher is called to such prophetic stands, but everyone who ministers the word of God must, by his words, use it to prepare the coming of God's kingdom of justice, love, truth and peace. If the Sunday homilist is to lay foundations for this kingdom, he must know where to start digging.

This dialogue between word and world or, better, the word that has come and the word to come (Ruysbroeck), will be the mainspring of the preacher's message. He will not have to answer all the questions, solve all the problems. Indeed, it is important that he admit the limits of his own knowledge and that of the experts of his day. The preacher is asked to bring the word of God received in scripture and tradition, in the broadest sense, to bear on current problems, and issues. He is not asked to deliver a political programme, a plan for social reform, a policy on cultural advancement. He is asked to offer a message of understanding, encouragement and hope both in this world and beyond it to those who live within these tensions. The preacher's long-term preparation for his task will bear fruit not in theological speculation, painstaking biblical exegesis or oratorical flamboyance. It will bring results in the word he gives the people — to have faith in life, trust in God, love of neighbour and hope in a world to come. That is how Irish people in 1986 described the qualities of a good homily.

The assembly

In the liturgy of the word God speaks to his people, stirs up their faith, brings to mind the great and small events of saving history, and nourishes their hearts with the bread of life, his divine wisdom. Everything in the liturgy of the word should help the people of God draw maximum benefit from sharing in this celebration, lead to a sincere offering of Eucharistic prayer and sacrifice and a fruitful reception of the sacrament. The word of God calls the Church together. The worshipping assembly becomes aware of its common bond in faith. It is prepared for life after the Eucharist to share fellowship and word together for the coming of the kingdom. These high ideals may not be found in every celebration. If heaven is paved with good intentions, it means we cannot get there without them.

Gathering, meeting, welcoming — all this is part of the preparation for the liturgy of the word. People need time to meet each other. When they enter the church, ushers or other ministers should be there to make them feel at home. Parents with children, in particular, should be made to feel especially welcome and, even more than others, perhaps, helped find a place to sit. In many churches ushers tend to be men of mature years, whose main function is often taking up the collection. There is need for a real ministry of welcome at the church door, one which women may be better fitted for. This will ease what is for many families an often stressful rush from bed to breakfast table to church. The more at ease they are in church, the easier it will be for them to enter into a spirit of prayer. In prayer they will be open to God's word. On the way out of church, a friendly greeting from parish clergy will encourage people to bring the word with them into daily life.

What does it mean to participate during the liturgy of the word? It involves many things; opening oneself to the word, recognising it as addressed to oneself, listening carefully as the word is proclaimed and explained, pondering what has been heard, and responding to it both individually and with others in prayer and praise and in a new way of living (*IGMR* 62; *DVD* 45-47).

During the liturgy of the word Christ speaks and his gathered people listen. The preacher serves Christ by addressing his word to a particular congregation. He serves the gathered people by creating the space for them to reflect and ponder what they have heard, by encouraging them to respond in their daily lives and by supporting them in that response.

Mary gives us the example of how we must listen to the word — she was blessed because she heard the word of God and kept it. So much so, the Word became flesh and dwelt with her, grew within her and with her, till he became a grown man. The same will happen in a spiritual way to those who come well-disposed to hear God's word at the Sunday Eucharist.

The principal liturgical sign in this celebration is the people of God themselves gathered for worship. Everything in the church should be arranged so that the people can participate fully. This means churches should be so arranged that eye contact between hearers of the word and those proclaiming it is possible. Long churches do not help this. If seating arrangements cannot be altered, it is even more important than is normally the case that public address systems be effective. The circular arrangement of the congregation, often preferred in modern church architecture, is most favourable to taking part in the liturgy of the word since it provides an opportunity for interaction between those in the body of the church with readers and preachers. In any event, the advice given in the national directory on church architecture, *Building and Reorganisation of Churches (BRC)*, could be carefully studied. Its provisions describe the best physical and pleasing conditions for hearing the word of God at Mass.

Ministers of the word

Those who minister the word by reading, chanting the psalm and preaching, do so in the name of Christ. He is acting through them in a special way. As a general rule readers in church should be invited to take part in this ministry on a regular basis, whether they are installed in the official ministry of lector or not. Those chosen for the task should have a natural talent for public reading, be persons of good character, and be prepared, at least, to study the scriptures and acquire any further skills they may need.

Readers need training for this ministry. Training will include an introduction to liturgy, scripture and public speaking. Following a short training programme they could begin by reading at weekday Masses. A definite standard is required before one is ready to read at Sunday Mass. In the *Survey on the Liturgy of the Word* 97% of adults and 78% of students questioned placed good reading as the first priority in making the lessons more appealing to listeners. Lay readers should not be used for 'symbolic' reasons. Unless they can communicate the message, they should not be asked to read. When they have proven their worth during a trial period, they could be assigned publicly to the office of reading for a specific period of time at a suitable Sunday Eucharist.

If enough readers volunteer, a panel can be set up and a rota system instituted. Those in this ministry will need continued help and guidance. They will benefit by regular meetings to study scripture, share notes and pray together. Proclaiming the word is not a mere technical performance. It presupposes an inner awareness of God's message, which will have to take root in the lives of those who hand it on.

If these steps are taken, the provisions of the *Liturgical Constitution* will be fulfilled when it says that readers and other ministers '...ought, therefore, to discharge their offices with the sincere piety and decorum demanded by so exalted a ministry and rightly expected of them by God's people. Consequently they must all be deeply imbued with the spirit of the liturgy, each in his own measure, and they must be trained to perform their functions in a correct and orderly manner' (SC 29).

In carrying out this office readers will not draw attention to themselves. The message is to be remembered, not the person who has read it. By voice, posture and dress the reader will convey the dignity and seriousness of the occasion. Dress should be dignified, quiet, without unnecessary ornament, neither too casual nor too formal. In this way the readers' bearing and appearance will not interfere with their wish to communicate God's word but will, rather, reinforce it.

Cantors

The cantor who sings or recites the psalm or canticle between the readings, like the reader, must have both talent and training. The responsorial psalm is the biblical passage which has least effect both on adult and student laity (only 28% of students, 58% of adults benefit from it). This suggests that the office of cantor needs to be developed so that the psalm is not recited but sung, as its nature suggests. In this way its true character will be more obvious and people will have the chance to reflect on the words while singing the response at least.

Readers of prayers

Those who read the prayers of the faithful will be prepared beforehand for this task. There is little point in someone with no experience of public speaking or of using a public address system, muttering inaudible words into a microphone. Reading the prayers, like reading the scriptures, is a serious liturgical office. Prayer is offered on behalf of the people. This will not be fully effective unless the people can hear the prayer and enter into its sentiments. If one of a panel of regular readers is not given the task, it helps if the person chosen has an opportunity for rehearsal before Mass, using the microphone if needed.

3

Signs and symbols

The Lectionary

As with other materials used in worship, it should be of good physical quality, its binding in good condition. An ancient Celtic tradition enshrines the books of scripture in sumptuous cases. This tradition lives on today when people provide a rich ornamental cover for the lectionary, which protects the book and enhances its appearance. A separate book of the gospels is recommended (*DVD* 36).

It is even more important that ministers of the word understand the structure and purpose of the Lectionary. The *General Introduction to the Lectionary for Mass* (second edition) has been read by 50% of Irish priests. It deserves detailed study as do other works which spell out its underlying plan in greater detail. The bishops of Vatican II asked that 'The treasures of the Bible ... be opened up more lavishly so that a richer fare may be provided for the faithful at the table of God's word' (*SC* 51). The current Lectionary is the answer to this request. Over a three-year cycle the Sunday lessons provide for the reading of most of the New Testament and a substantial part of the Old.

The readings have been arranged according to a two-tiered plan. At one level they follow the liturgical year. Within this framework, for much of the time they follow, as continuous readings, the order of books concerned, mainly those of the New Testament. In ordinary time the Old Testament reading harmonises with the gospel, indicating together a central message for the day.

The significance of any passage read has to be worked out with these two points of reference in mind: its place in a particular book and its reference to a particular moment in the liturgical year. For example, the account of Jesus' Transfiguration can be read from one angle during Lent, from another on the Feast of the Transfiguration; the account of the Passion will have one resonance on Good Friday, another on the Feast of the Exaltation of the Cross. At the same time the vision of a particular author will enter into the picture. The Passion narrative of each of the four evangelists has its own emphasis. This will affect the presentation of these gospels and their use in preaching.

In short, a study of scripture is not all that is required of ministers of the word; they must also have a knowledge of the Lectionary and the link between lesson and liturgical cycle of feasts. If this need were met, there would be less reason on the part of some to regret the passage of older programmes of catechetical instruction as a framework for preaching. As the *Introduction to the Lectionary* points out, celebration also teaches faith. 'This finds expression in the Lectionary of the Roman Missal, which can thus be justly regarded as a catechetical teaching aid. The Order of Readings for Mass offers an appropriate scriptural presentation of the most important of all that was done and said in the history of salvation' (*DVD* 61).

In other words, there is a programme of instruction laid down in the Lectionary based on the liturgical year and the inner structure of the gospels in particular. This provides for the presentation of all the main mysteries of the faith — not in the particular sequence of post-Tridentine catechetics, but in the more ancient order of liturgical celebration and evangelical narrative. A quick glance at this implicit programme indicates how the main mysteries of faith are remembered and pondered on.

The principal moments of liturgical celebration are the Paschal cycle from Ash Wednesday to Pentecost and the Christmas cycle from Advent to the Baptism of our Lord. Following this in chronological sequence, we begin with the Old Testament anticipation of Christ, his conception, birth and manifestation to the world, the announcement of his public ministry. The Easter cycle brings us to the core of the Paschal Mystery, with its

59

constant focus through Lent on the essential message of Jesus, and its climax in his death and resurrection. The period after Easter can be followed with John as an extended meditation on the Risen Lord or with the Acts of the Apostles as a reflection on the Church. The celebration of Pentecost focuses on the gift of the Spirit as completing the Paschal Mystery, while the return to ordinary time with Trinity Sunday brings us back to origins and forward to Trinitarian kingdom, the ultimate crown of all effort.

The Synoptic Gospels form the central thread of reading in ordinary time. In their turn, Matthew, Mark and Luke provide many occasions for both the celebration and presentation of the principal aspects of Christian faith over the three-year cycle.

This cursory glance at the Lectionary's structure merely serves to show the importance of getting a grasp of its layout and of relating its contents to this framework. There is ample opportunity for linking other aspects of ministry with the Sunday celebration, notably the catechetical programmes in use in schools as well as other events of significance to the community. On the other hand if too many 'special cause Sundays' (e.g. temperance, peace, justice, the unborn) are added to the liturgical cycle, its own inner significance and formative power will be lost. As far as possible the liturgical cycle of readings should be observed and their riches revealed to meet the needs of the faithful.

The use of pamphlets, sheets of paper, missalettes for the proclamation of God's word is unacceptable. It is neither fitting nor helpful to good celebration. The Lectionary and Gospel book should be used for this purpose. They should be handled with a reverence which expresses and deepens the faith of the community in God's word. Deacon or reader carries the book solemnly in procession at the end as at the beginning of Mass. It is revered with a kiss, honoured with incense. The homilist often preaches with open book before him. It is left on the lectern throughout Mass, never pushed aside, and during the week it is placed in a prominent position near the altar in remembrance of God's gift of his word.

The Ambo

The ambo or lectern is part of the essential furnishing of a church. In itself it should be a sign of what it is used for — proclaiming God's word. It should be high enough for the ministers of the word to be clearly seen and heard in every part of the church. 'The position, distinctive design and form of the ambo should express its relationship to the altar and the dignity of the word of God' (BRC 5.4). It should be sufficiently large to accommodate several ministers and have adequate lighting and sound equipment.

The lectern is the correct place for readings, chanting the responsorial psalm and preaching. The celebrant may introduce the creed and prayers of the faithful from either the lectern or president's chair. Other rites are carried out elsewhere — at the president's chair, another lectern or choir platform. Reserving one place for God's word emphasises its importance. To use it for other purposes such as giving directions to the assembly or reading notices trivialises the word and robs it of importance.

Introducing the lessons

Many of the people surveyed (89% of adults, 74% of students) suggested short introductions to the readings at Mass as a help in explaining their message. This request is understandable since at Mass the scripture passages are always heard outside their literary context. Introductions to the readings should be brief, about three sentences, not short homilies. When introducing the first lesson, it can be helpful to show how it links in with the gospel. Skill is required in composing these introductions. Some assistance can be found in liturgical resource material provided by *Scripture in Church, Intercom* and other publications.

Public address systems

Public address systems should not be taken for granted. They should be designed with the acoustic needs of a church in mind. When people complain that they cannot hear in church, it is usually not so much a problem of volume as of confusion of sounds. This arises when hard surfaces re-echo sounds over a period of time so that the same sound can continue for several seconds, drowning what follows. The time it takes a loud sound to die down in an enclosed space is called reverberation time. Professional skill, that of an acoustic consultant, not an architect or electronics engineer, is required to design a sound system which will keep the reverberation time at an appropriate level. With the right technology, most church buildings can be made suitable for public speech.

Microphones, too, have their own different qualities and capabilities. Priests will be familiar with those in use in their own churches. But when lay people are introduced to the reading ministry, whether as members of a panel or on special occasions, they will need guidance. They should be shown how to use the microphone in place and should be given a chance to rehearse. Otherwise, little of what they say will be heard.

Like any machine, public address systems need to be checked and serviced on a regular basis. The congregation, or at least those members most closely involved with the liturgy, may be encouraged to report on the functioning of the public address system so that faults, whether human or electronic, can be identified and remedied.

Silences

The liturgy of the word provides for distinct moments of silence so that all may reflect on God's word. These occur at the end of each reading, when the reader remains for a few moments with head bowed. If this has not been the custom to date, the reader or presiding celebrant would be advised to invite the audience to listen — for some word, perhaps, in the passage just read, which has struck them — and let the Spirit speak it once more in silence of their hearts. Such periods of silence are expected after each reading and the homily (*IGMR* 23). The homilist could sit down at this point and join with the people in a slightly longer period of reflection.

Periods of silence are important; without them the liturgy will become a succession of readings, prayers, acclamations, a non-stop journey from start to finish without time to take stock. If this happens, the contemplative dimension of prayer — or just the space within which people can bring their own thoughts before God — will be lost.

4

Rites

The opening rites of the Mass are an important preliminary to celebrating the word. Whenever suitable and possible there should be an entrance procession with thurible, cross, candle-bearers, book of the gospels held high, and all ministers taking part in the celebration. Music and song, whether accompanying a procession or not, are also important in creating an atmosphere of recollection and prayer among the assembled people. If there is a procession, the book of the gospels can be placed on the altar as a sign of its link with the Eucharistic bread, while the readers, with the other ministers, take their places in the sanctuary or close to it.

The principal celebrant's opening word of welcome will usually include some reference to a central theme of celebration, a theme which will be echoed in the readings, from the topic of the homily, and for intercession in the prayer of the faithful.

The penance rite can carry this reflection forward by basing the examination of conscience on it, using suitable phrases of the day's scripture in the invocation of mercy. The invitation to pray at the collect could also echo this note.

The lessons

It is better to have separate readers for each reading. This adds variety to the presentation. The person who takes the first reading should pause at the end to allow the congregation to reflect on what they have heard. If this is a novelty, one may have to explain the reason for silence, to encourage the listeners to focus on a word that has struck them in the lesson.

Preferably, the psalm should be sung or read by another person (*IGMR* 36, 67, 90). It may be easier to sing if the cantor uses a text and music familiar to the congregation from the *Simple Gradual* or *Graduale Romanum*. Except, perhaps, in children's Masses, the proper proclamation of the word demands that it be entrusted to adults.

The gospel

The minister of the gospel is the deacon. Where there is no deacon, a priest concelebrating other than the president will read the gospel. It is, indeed, incorrect for the principal celebrant to do this if a deacon or priest is celebrating with him (*IGMR* 34).

The gospel is, of course, the most important of the readings. It should be surrounded by greater ceremonial. When a separate book is used for the gospel reading, it will be carried in procession to the lectern. If space is limited in the sanctuary, a 'roundabout' route for the procession may be considered. Processions need room to process! When one lectionary is used for all three readings, it remains on the lectern. Servers with candles and thurifer lead the minister to the ambo. The candles are held on either side. The minister incenses the book. The book itself is kissed after the reading and may be raised high before the congregation as they make their acclamation. All these signs of respect are addressed to Christ present in his gospel (*IGMR* 9).

The gospel acclamation is sung as the procession takes place. it is intended to be a joyful shout of welcome to Christ the Lord who is about to speak to us. It can be extended, when appropriate, by adding additional versicles to the chant between the Alleluia. Alleluia is more for singing than for saying. The *General Instruction* says it may be omitted if not sung. However, it is much better included and sung both before and after the gospel's proclamation.

The homily

The homily is an important and integral part of the liturgy, not an optional extra. As it is of such importance, it will be dealt with in a separate section below.

The profession of faith

The recitation of the Nicene Creed (or, in certain circumstances, the Apostles' Creed) is part of the liturgy of the word for Sundays (*IGMR* 43,44). It is not an optional extra, liable to be dropped if the readings or the homily are lengthy. In reciting the Creed, priest and people reaffirm their faith in God's word, not just as it has been proclaimed and preached at this Mass, but as it has traditionally been proclaimed and celebrated through the ages.

The prayer of the faithful

The prayer of the faithful should be introduced and concluded by the presiding celebrant (*IGMR* 47), the petitions by a deacon, cantor or other assistant. In the prayer of the faithful the people exercise their priestly function by praying for all humanity. The petitions offered may reflect the needs of the local community as well as themes occurring in the liturgy of the day. Where possible, it is helpful if these petitions are composed by the local community, guided by the priest. However, they should follow correct liturgical style and be prepared in advance. The *General Instruction* suggests a particular sequence; the needs of the Church (local and/or universal); civil authorities, the salvation of the whole world, those oppressed by any need, the local community. It also makes good sense to incorporate what many call the Parish List of the Dead into the prayer of the faithful rather than including it with the parish notices. The living as well as the dead of the parish should be prayed for, especially those who have celebrated sacraments such as baptism, first communion and matrimony.

5

The practice of preaching

While the scripture readings, especially the gospel, get a good response, especially from adults, and most people (84%) want to hear a good sermon, 57% are only occasionally helped by the Sunday homily. With certain groups of people, such as the young, the single, the better educated, the city dwellers, the proportion is even lower. In terms of successful celebration this is an unhappy situation. If one were to imagine a congregation which mirrored exactly the sample taken in the survey, one would find a gradual surge of interest from first to second reading, and then on to the gospel. This drops away at the homily. That which should be the climax of the liturgy of the word, the message which should awaken faith for the celebration of the Eucharist, has almost a reverse effect for many. People 'switch off' rather than 'switch on'. Whether this is obvious within any particular celebration or not, it must have a subconscious effect on the atmosphere in church, and make it difficult for people to join fully in what follows.

This is one more among many reasons why the preparation and delivery of the Sunday sermon is so central to liturgical ministry. Responsibility is not exclusively the priest's. Those who find the homily useful are generally people who consider membership of the Catholic Church important, who pray more frequently, who attend Mass and the sacraments more regularly. If one comes prepared, if one is hungry for the word, then what is presented will be more easily relished. Nonetheless, the less careful sheep, the less wise virgins are part of the community. Many want to hear a good homily. This suggests they are open to the word, to deeper conversion, to more active sharing in the Eucharist. There is an opportunity here not to be missed.

A partnership in the word

The very name homily, or *homilia* (Gk) suggests being together, intercourse, converse, dealings with others, hence instruction and meeting. The homily is dialogue, or arises from dialogue. The kind of dialogue suggested in the following pages has the mysterious character referred to by the Flemish mystic Jan Van Ruysbroeck: 'The God in the depths of us ... receives the God who comes to us'. The God of life, of history, of secular existence, meets the God made flesh in Jesus Christ. The homilist is both the field where this encounter takes place and its privileged observer. From it he will draw light and fire for his people, and for himself.

This view of homily may be put in other words borrowed from the US Bishops when they describe preaching the word of God as '... a scriptural interpretation of human existence which enables a community to recognise God's active presence, to respond to that presence in faith through liturgical word and gesture, and beyond the liturgical assembly, through a life lived in conformity to the Gospel ...' (*Fulfilled*, 29). The word of God truly proclaimed arouses living faith. From that faith flows eucharistic praise and sacrificial offering. This goes on when liturgy is ended, in a life of prayer, fellowship, witness and public expression of the faith that saves.

Because it is an intrinsic part of liturgical celebration the proclamation of the word is not a mere exercise in public speaking. There are some similarities: one person speaks and a larger number of individuals listen; various backgrounds and levels of commitment among the listeners mean that the effective preacher draws upon mass communication techniques. Communication is largely through the medium of the spoken word, and the preacher often uses amplification devices such as microphone systems. However, the preacher does not have the same relationship with the gathered community that the public speaker has with his audience. He does not speak as the informed to the uninformed. Both preacher and listener share the common bond of baptism, and have the Spirit of God within them.

While each preacher will take his own soundings among his people, the *Survey on the Liturgy of the Word* provides some useful indications of people's expectations of the homily. To explain the purpose of the homily, students used phrases such as 'to explain the gospel in modern terms,'; 'to relate God to our lives'; 'to outline rules for living'; 'to improve our faith in God'. Adults said the sermon should 'explain the readings in everyday language'; 'help to keep God's teachings in mind'; 'encourage people to improve their way of life'. The emphasis overall was on linking word with life.

This same stress appeared again when people were asked why a particular homily had appealed to them. Students said: 'it brought home a message'; 'it showed that God remembers us'; 'it related to me and my situation'. Adults said 'it taught me a lesson'; 'it made me aware'; 'it was encouraging'; 'it helped me recall earlier teachings'; 'it was relevant to present-day issues'. The desire to build a bridge between word and life, or to illumine life better by the light of the gospel is reflected in many priests' opinions on the same subject: 'to bring good news relevant to people's lives'; 'to encourage people in their Christian lives'; 'to stimulate people into putting the word into action'. Preachers who work within this frame of reference have a good start in getting their message across.

Preparation

Each preacher has his own style and his own way of preparing. However, all preachers must prepare. There are a thousand and one excuses for not preparing. Many of them are understandable, few are valid. What follows are some guidelines which a preacher may find useful.

Time: Spread your preparation over the week rather than rushing it at the last minute. Four or five hours is not too much to spend at a task which plays such an important role in the climax of a priest's week, Sunday Mass. Fulton Sheen normally spent ten hours preparing a ten-minute talk. There are many demands on a priest's time. Only emergencies can compare with this. Set aside a regular time each week for preparation, a time when you are fresh and can think clearly. The 18% of priests who prepare 'throughout the week' probably have it right in that respect, provided quality time is given to the job each day. Go somewhere you cannot be disturbed. (If this is not possible at home, then maybe spend a day away in a friend's house to have the necessary peace and quiet.) Begin early in the week so as to allow time for further thought, revision of your script and getting full control of your material.

Prayer: As preacher you represent Christ in the gathered community. The 57% of priests who bring preaching into their prayer realise they have to put their ministry into the hands of the Lord and rely on him. He preaches as they talk. In prayerful reflection on the liturgical texts the Spirit will bring inspiration — topics, words, incidents — to mind which will help the sermon, give it a power far in excess of the speaker's gifts.

Choosing a topic: In many ways this is the most important aspect of preparation. Three quarters of the clergy draw their topics from the readings, especially the gospels. In doing this they follow the liturgical plan which sees the main theme for reflection in the gospel, focused in ordinary time by the Old Testament pericope. However, it is not enough to recognise this. There can be several ways of looking at any gospel passage. We should also reflect on our personal experience, the experience of those we have met of late, the current affairs of our community and world at large. Doing this may recall questions, insights, epigrams, anecdotes or issues which illustrate or run parallel to the scriptural message for the day. This confluence of inner, worldly and scriptural word (all with the same author) will provide an agenda for preaching.

This may be doctrinal — if someone raised a doctrinal question; it may be scriptural — if we felt challenged by a word from scripture; it may be moral, social or political (in the broad sense) — if the spark came in those quarters. What matters is that we listen to the word not merely in scripture and its tradition but also in our hearts, in those of our people and of the world around us, and illumine one by the other. Life brings scripture into the twentieth century; the biblical message unravels the paradox and puzzle of life. The word which saves is a sentence: the subject comes from life; the predicate from tradition; the verb from the heart.

The classic example of this approach was Jesus' first sermon in his home town. People were asking questions about the miracles he had been working. He attended the village synagogue on the Sabbath and read from the prophet Isaiah: ' "The Spirit of the Lord is upon me.... He has sent me to proclaim release to the captives and recovering of sight to the blind, to set at liberty those who are oppressed, to proclaim the acceptable year of the Lord' (*Is 61:1-2*) .... And he began to say to them, "Today this scripture has been fulfilled in your hearing ..." ' (*Lk 4:18-21*). The pattern is clear: people are asking questions; the scripture is proclaimed; from this inner awareness of the Spirit Jesus interprets scripture and answers the questions. Indeed the rest of the familiar story shows how sensitive he was to popular feeling and how he addressed it in his sermon, even at the risk of incurring the people's anger.

Commentaries: Do some research to see what scriptural commentaries have to say about the readings. The most popular with Irish priests is *Scripture in Church*, used by 29%. It comes in magazine format. Commentaries are brief — it might be wise to dig a little deeper using William Barclay's single volume series (used by 8% of clergy), or the Veritas/Glazier *Good News Studies* (1983), or any of the standard one-volume commentaries. Quite often a commentator will throw up a word or a phrase or parallel reference which will catch your imagination or give a fresh angle to a text. The same can occur when you pursue cross-references and marginal notes provided, for example, in the *New Jerusalem Bible*. Such research enables the concerns of the inspired authors and their communities to become clearer to you and will give an edge to your use of scripture.

Tradition: As a preacher you also represent the wider Catholic tradition. When you decide on a message, check current Church or theological teaching on the subject. This can provide a broader context or a new slant on a jaded theme. Share with your community the experience of Christians throughout the ages. Don't let them become slaves of the present moment. The Church has been here for 2000 years. That is a mine of experience to draw on.

Vision: Have a vision of the community that you seek to form. The effective homily is one that has an impact upon the way in which we live our lives. If you want a serving, apostolic community, for example, this will figure regularly in your preaching by way of examples from parish or other life, or by invitation to involvement.

Illustration: Having reflected on the scriptures and your experience and decided on a topic, you will fill out your message. You know you have to get attention from the start, so announce your theme, develop it, link it with the Eucharist and with life, and end, if possible, with a memorable phrase. With this in mind, it is helpful to collect articles, cuttings, quotes, stories, personal flashes of insight, significant scriptural or other passages. Filed under subject headings, this can be your own data bank of sermon illustrations. It can be helpful to use collections of homilies and homily services, not to provide the substance of your talk, but the apt phrase or telling quotation.

Whatever value published sources have, in the eyes of the people the illustrations they find most suitable are those drawn from your own personal life (adults 65%, students 56%) and from those of the people (adults 57%, students 45%).* If these can be put in story form the impact will be all the greater (with adults, 72%, with students, 70%). In fact, such methods are considered effective by most priests. For those already using them it will be a question of refining their use, perhaps by testing out

---

* These figures were obtained by combining the responses ('very effective' and 'effective') as found in the full reports on adults' and students' attitudes to the liturgy of the word (pp. 16,17). Hence the discrepancy with the table, pp. 104-5; the summary report gives figures only for 'very effective' techniques.

beforehand with a sermon preparation group or with fellow priests. In the longer term, further training in public speaking might give more bite to both composition and delivery of homilies.

Preparation groups: The lines of communication between you and your people must be open and active. One of the most difficult aspects of successful communication to achieve in the preaching context is that of feedback. Yet 'What is communicated is not what is said, but it is what is heard' (*Fulfilled*, 4). Feedback is, of course, restricted in any sustained way with a large congregation during the celebration of the liturgy of the word itself. The preacher can, however, establish effective feedback channels before and after preaching.

In fact, more than half the priests questioned in the *Survey on the Liturgy of the Word* said they had asked a lay person's opinion of a recent sermon, but it appears that only a limited range of people was consulted. Some 22% of the clergy have used organised groups of laity to help prepare the sermon; 90% of them found this helpful. 30% of the clergy have discussed the readings with parish groups.

The survey does not reveal which type of group proved most successful. However, common sense and the general principles governing group behaviour suggest that a group of seven or eight, broadly representative of the parish, which changes from time to time while meeting on a weekly basis will prove more effective. The results of the *Survey* suggest that it is important that such groups reflect the broad spectrum of the parish. A fan club is of little use.

You will, of course, work out your own approach with such a group. One possible method is as follows. Begin with prayer that the proclaimed word may be heard in the parish community. Then review last week's homily, looking for feedback and evaluation. Then examine the scriptural texts for the next Sunday Mass. Begin with the gospel and move to the first reading. The second reading should be examined last. It is important not to begin by explaining these texts; rather you should listen as others share what they understand and do not understand, and what encourages or challenges them in the texts to be proclaimed. Make careful note of these concerns; they will help to focus your homily. In discussion the vision that the texts offer to the Christian community should emerge. Once again listen carefully as others share their experiences of trying to live according to this vision. At this stage you could usefully try out some ideas for your homily and get reactions. Introductions to the readings could also usefully be scripted at this time. If readers are present at the meeting their role should also be considered. Communication is enhanced when readers and preachers have a common understanding.

Putting it down on paper

One piece of advice comes loud and clear from the survey. Have a clear message, if you want an effective sermon, say 86% of adults, 66% of students — and 94% of priests agree.* Again, this raises questions as to whether priests are achieving this on a regular basis in their preaching. Regular feedback will keep the preacher informed on this point.

How to achieve it? First, define your topic clearly. Express it in a simple sentence. For example, the 32nd Sunday of Year B has the gospel story of the widow's mite (*Mk 12:38-44*) matched by the story from the Elijah cycle of the window of Zarephath (*1 K 17:10-16*). One way to define the topic for that Sunday is 'God loves a generous giver.' This is the simple message. This same theme can be used in the introduction to the homily, the development, the link with the Eucharist, the conclusion.

If you start writing about mid-week, preparing a text or the main points, you will have time to revise. This is essential. A day later you will be more objective about what you have written. You will see surplus words and sentences, see yourself trying to put too much information into one homily, notice yourself wandering up favourite sideroads, or flogging familiar hobbyhorses. Composition early in the week with later revision is one way to keep yourself to the main point. Whether you write

---

* These figures come from the full reports, pp. 16, 17.

out your text in full or simply jot down points with useful thoughts and phrases, make sure you write for speaking. One way of doing this is to speak your words out loud. If they sound right, write them down for memory's sake. Use short simple sentences. Avoid theological jargon and a literary style.

Edit: When the time comes for revision edit your text for clarity and length. Make sure you have a striking opinion, interesting illustrations, preferably in story form. A touch of humour goes a long way. Your homily should link to the rest of the liturgy. See that it relates to the readings, links up with the introductory words at the beginning of Masses, opens out readily to the prayer of the faithful and leads into the Eucharistic Prayer.

You might like to check whether it will meet people's expectations. Students and adults surveyed listed the following as qualities they appreciate in a good sermon. So, is it *interesting*? (adults 24%, students 30%). Does it reflect the priest's own *experience*? (adults 15%, students 12%). Is it *short*? (adults 15%, students 12%) — short means not more than ten minutes say adults 69%, students 61%. Is it *relevant* to everyday life? (adults 14%, students 20%); Is it to the *point*? (adults 14%, students 15%). Does it tell a *story*? (adults 8%, students 17%). If you edit your homily on Thursday or Friday you will have time to make changes necessary to meet these requirements.

Are you ready? Probably never! However, take heart. It is not you who preaches but Christ who speaks through you. All you can do is prepare and deliver the message. He must bring the increase. But there are signs that you are ready to speak: if you care about your homily, if you believe what you say really matters, if you clearly see how you hope people will change as a result of your words.

Delivering the homily

Preparation is an aid to preaching. It must not limit you as you relate to the assembled community. A script may help this but can never be a substitute for it. If you can, speak without notes.

Speak to people that you care about — on something that you care about. Share your beliefs and your hopes for this community. Encourage as well as inform. Speak clearly and loudly (mentioned by 17% of adults, 11% of students).

The congregation should be active during the homily. Challenge them to think, reflect and decide. Avoid always speaking to the same group in church. (Not everyone is married or part of a family, for example.) Some talks could be addressed to single people, to the old, the sick, the bored.

Keep your homily short. Five to seven minutes is the usual time the average congregation will remain interested. Do not try to say everything on the subject. The longer a homily, the less will be remembered. Conversely, if you limit what you have to say but what you say is relevant, that little may have great impact.

When appropriate, use lay resources to enrich your preaching. Invite a parent to talk about family prayer, a social worker on the task of caring for the sick, a returned emigrant on the need for support, a St Vincent de Paul member on the plight of the poor. Variety of voice and face can keep interest alive in a congregation. To some extent you are in competition with radio and TV. Something can be learned from their techniques. Moreover, the use of specialised experience and knowledge in 'the age of the expert' can make the message more imperative. Those who help you with the sharing of the word will have to be carefully chosen, given due notice and encouraged to prepare in advance. If unused to public speaking they may need some rehearsal.

If you feel threatened by competition from the media, remember that people are more interested in their own backyard than in Buffalo or Baluchistan. If you can show how Jacob's ladder is firmly grounded in that backyard, you will have done most of your work.

Conclusion

At the risk of unnecessary repetition — some final suggestions from the laity to their preachers. Asked to give advice to a priest, the most frequent comments from adults were: keep it short;

speak clearly; keep to the point; prepare the sermon well; relate the sermon to everyday life; make it interesting. Students replied: Be brief, don't drag on; make it interesting; refer to everyday experiences of the congregation; stick to the point; make it humorous; speak clearly; get to know young people and their interests.

All of this has been said before. Its repetition will highlight the place of the homily in a priest's ministry. It is not something separate from his daily dealing with people, those he visits or meets on the street and in parish groups. *Homily* in its original Greek sense means 'being with people', chatting with them, dialogue. From this dialogue will come the living questions, issues and problems the preacher will respond to in his Sunday address. If he listens carefully, he will often hear not merely the question but the answer and sometimes the telling phrase which sums it all up. From lively conversation, living dialogue, comes good preaching and joyful Eucharist.

The life of Mary of Nazareth captures such openness to the word, to need, to question. In the Visitation, she sensed Elizabeth's need, met it, and from that encounter flowed the Magnificat. At Cana, she sensed the anguish of the hosts. She commented on it, and from this came her Son's first miracle. In prayer she listened to God. When the angel came with his invitation, her response was one of acceptance and generosity.

'Behold, I am the handmaid of the Lord; let it be to me according to your word' (*Lk 1:38*). Mary was blessed because she heard the word of God and kept it (Lk 11:28). Because she listened and responded in faith, in her the Word was fully made flesh (Jn 1:14).

Part II

The proclamation of the word assessed

*A sociological study of attitudes
among clergy and people to the
celebration of the word in Ireland, 1986*

by
Ann Breslin SSL, PhD

Introduction

It is a truism to say that the most frequent occasion for communication between priests and laity is at Sunday Mass, during which the means of communication are usually the various elements of the liturgy of the word: the readings, psalm, gospel and homily.

It was to explore the effectiveness of transmitting the liturgy of the word, particularly the delivery of the homily, that the Irish Commission for Liturgy requested the Council for Research and Development to carry out a survey on the liturgy of the word. This was intended to elicit the opinions of priests and laity and, based upon its findings, the Commission hoped to be able to make some recommendations about preparing both priests and people to develop the potential of the sermon[2] as a means of transmitting the word of God and the values of the gospel.

Survey design

Since the aim of the survey was to elicit the opinions of priests and laity on various aspects of the liturgy of the word, with a special emphasis on the homily, it was important to have a random sample of priests and laity so that the responses could be generalised to the population as a whole.

---

[2]The term *sermon* was used for *homily* in the survey as it was found to be the term most frequently used by the laity.

Random sample of priests (N = 425)

The *Irish Catholic Directory* was the source from which was drawn a random sample of priests that approximated to the total number of priests in Ireland in regard to age structure and to location of parishes. Care was taken too, to plan for adequate representation of numbers in densely populated areas.

Postal questionnaires were sent to 636 randomly selected priests, and a high (67%) return rate was received. Thus, the opinions expressed by the priests, as reported in this survey, may be regarded as representative of responses from the Irish diocesan clergy.

Age structure

Just over one fifth of the priests were in the 'young' category (24-40 years), 50% were in the 'middle' group (41-60 years) and over a quarter were aged 61-88 years. Over one third were parish priests and almost six in ten were curates. A small percentage named themselves 'in other ministries'.

Location of parishes

More than half (56%) of the priests worked in rural areas, approximately one in five in small towns, and a quarter in large towns or in urban areas.

Random sample of laity (N = 428)

The selection of the laity was undertaken by a process of stratified random sampling. First, we selected areas in Northern Ireland and in the Republic that corresponded to the three categories: city, town, rural. Within these areas we selected parishes or sections of parishes where we might expect to find different socio-economic groups, e.g. professional people, blue collar workers, unskilled workers, etc. Within such parish areas we then randomly selected from parish registers pre-determined numbers of respondents to form a representative pattern of each area as a whole.

Gender

Although the original selected number comprised equal numbers of men and women, more women than men were willing to complete the questionnaire. Thus the final sample was composed of two thirds women (N = 256) and one third men (N = 172), an imbalance which ought to be taken into account when interpreting the results.

Marital status and age

About three in ten respondents were single, over a half were married and the remaining one eighth were widowed or separated. Almost half were aged under 40, one third were in the age group 41-60 and one sixth were over 60 years old.

Location

Almost half (47%) of the respondents were from rural areas, one fifth from small/medium towns and one third from large towns and cities. This distribution approximated to that of the priests already described above.

Sample of Students (N = 207)

It was considered important to consult students who were in their final year in post-primary school, and would soon be the young adults in their parishes. Four comprehensive schools were selected (two in Northern Ireland and two in the Republic). In both cases, urban and rural locations were found.

The questionnaire was administered by the Project Director to a total of 207 students, aged 16-17 years. The students were assured of anonymity and confidentiality, and from the Director's personal experience, the students gave the questionnaire careful consideration and a serious response.

Interviews

Since the method of consulting the laity was by an interview-questionnaire, groups of interviewers were trained in the appropriate techniques. Each interviewer carried a letter of introduction from the Director of Research and Development, and from the parishioner's Parish Priest. The respondents were assured of the confidentiality and anonymity of their scripts, which would be analysed by computer in Research and Development. It was made clear to them that no priest or other member of the parish would read their responses. The interviewers carried out their task with a high degree of professionalism and thoroughness. However, despite their best efforts, some of the selected parishioners were not immediately available, and a few were unwilling to complete the questionnaire. In all, 428 parishioners' questionnaires were processed.

Section I

The laity and the liturgy of the word

When asked to state whether the liturgy of the word gave inspiration for reflection, the adults' responses were as follows:

Inspiration	A lot	Some-thing	Not much	Nothing at all
First reading	18%	54%	23%	5%
Second reading	17%	59%	19%	4%
Responsorial psalm	20%	38%	29%	13%
Gospel	52%	40%	5%	3%

Comments made by adults	No. of times mentioned	% of responses (N=112)
'The readings and the gospel are very important'	13	12%
'The gospel is the only important reading'	13	12%
'The readings are too far removed from reality'	8	7%
'The responsorial psalm and gospel are relevant and give guidelines for living'	7	6%

The students' responses were as follows:

Inspiration	A lot	Something	Not much	Nothing at all
First reading	8%	30%	44%	18%
Second reading	7%	33%	43%	18%
Responsorial psalm	6%	22%	42%	30%
Gospel	32%	41%	15%	12%

Comments made by students	No. of times mentioned	% of responses (N=70)
'The gospel has more bearing than the other readings'	14	20%
'The message in the readings is not explained well enough'	13	19%
'Responsorial psalm is too repetitive and irrelevant'	10	14%
'Repetitive sermons and readings'	6	9%

Understanding the structure of the readings

A general question revealed a need for more education of the laity in the relevance of the liturgy of the word. The question was: 'Have you been helped to understand why we have three readings and a psalm at Mass on Sundays?' The responses to this question were as follows:

Adults		Students	
Yes	No	Yes	No
13%	87%	5%	95%

A high degree of interest was expressed by both groups in response to the question: 'Would you like help in this regard?'

	Adults			Students	
	Yes	No		Yes	No
	80%	20%		74%	26%

Both adults and students gave similar priority to two ways of helping them to improve their understanding of the readings:

	Adults	Students
'A few words of introduction'	89%	74%
'Good readers'	97%	78%

Interest in the readings

A specific question about interest in the first and second readings elicited the following responses:

	Always/ Usually	Some- times	Rarely/ Never
'I often look at the readings before Mass, so I'll know what is coming'			
Adults:	20%	23%	56%
Students:	7%	19%	73%
'I often look at the readings after Mass so as to think more about them'			
Adults:	7%	16%	77%
Students:	3%	4%	93%
'I find I can listen to the readings'			
Adults:	78%	18%	4%
Students:	*	*	*
'I generally understand what the readings mean'			
Adults:	74%	22%	4%
Students:	43%	42%	15%

'I find it difficult to listen to the
readings'
Adults: 6%   33%   61%
Students: *   *   *

'I generally don't understand
what some of the readings mean'
Adults: 8%   35%   57%
Students: *   *   *

'The readings mean nothing
to me'
Adults: 14%   19%   67%
Students: *   *   *

* *Students were not asked this question.*

Section II

Training in preaching

A number of questions to priests focused on their perceptions of the training they had received in their seminaries. Priests of all ages were almost evenly divided in their opinions of the usefulness of their seminary training for preaching: almost half (48%) regarded it as having been useful in regard to 'content' and a similar proportion (48%) were satisfied that the training 'techniques' had been of benefit.

The positive comments were of a general nature, for example 'We received good guidelines' but the groups who were dissatisfied gave more explicit reasons, with two major points of emphasis; 'too theoretical' and 'insufficient practice'. About one fifth of these focused on the gap between training and 'reality'. They used phrases such as, 'Too theoretical, artificial, academic, not related to real life; no contact with parish life' and 'There were too many students for individual attention; we had little practice, as we had sermons only once or twice a year'.

Present adequacy of trainig

When the priests were asked if at present they feel adequately trained to give a good sermon, more than half (57%) were positive, although more than a quarter (28%) were 'not sure'. The most frequent comments were: 'Experience has taught me' and 'I've learnt by trial and error'. There were no significant differences in the responses when analysed by priests' age or location of parish.

Courses attended since ordination

Only four in ten priests had, since ordination, attended a course on preaching. Of these, 80% had found the course or courses 'helpful' or 'very helpful'.

Some comments made by this group (N = 139) who had found the course 'helpful' were:

	Number of times mentioned	% of responses (N = 139)
1. 'I recognised faults in my preaching and changed accordingly'...'My technique was criticised and that helped me to improve'.	37	22%
2. 'I did a course at the Communications Centre'; 'I did a course using TV etc.'	20	12%

We found that the majority (57%) of those who had attended a course were in the 'middle' age category (41-60 years). Only 17% of the younger priests (24-40 years) had done so, as had 28% of the older men (61+ years).

Willingness to attend a course on preaching

Although only four in ten priests had actually attended a course on preaching, the willingness to do so was much more marked, with almost two thirds (64%) expressing a wish for further training. Those who wanted further training were found to be proportionately more from the youngest group: (almost 80% of those aged under 40, by comparison with approximately 70% of the 'middle' group (41-60 years) and 40% of the oldest group).

Thus the findings indicate that, whereas younger priests

expressed a wish for further training, by comparison with the older age groups, fewer of these younger priests had in fact attended such a course.

Almost half of the respondents agreed that such 'further training' should be organised at diocesan level. However, approximately one in six priests opted for this training to be organised at national or at deanery level.

Preaching resource centre

There was strong support (from over two thirds of the priests) for a preaching resource centre. In this case too, the emphasis was on providing such a centre at diocesan level.

When asked to name facilities desirable in such a centre, the highest proportion of responses (32%) approximated to: 'A library with books, videos, periodicals, sermons for various occasions, film strips'. More than one sixth of the responses referred to 'Professional staff and recording facilities'.

Section III

Perception of the sermon

Importance of Sermons

Over two thirds of the priests considered preaching to be 'Very Important' in their ministry, while approximately a quarter classified it as 'Important'. Among those who considered it 'Very Important', we noted a higher proportion (80%) of the oldest group, compared with 60% of the youngest group.

Function of sermons

The three groups surveyed (priests, lay adults, students) were asked, 'What do you think is the principal function of a sermon in the Sunday Mass?'. The responses below were given by the indicated percentages in each group. (Lower percentages than these were omitted.)

Principal function of the sermon

Priests	% of responses (N = 425)
'Instruct...educate...explain'	25%
'Bring Good News to be relevant to people's lives'	16%
'Inspire...encourage people in their Christian lives'	13%
'Challenge...stimulate people into putting word into action'	11%

Adults	% of responses (N = 411)
'Explain the readings in everyday language'	16%
'To give a simple message'	12%
'To keep God's teachings in mind'	10%
'Encourage people to improve ways of living'	10%

Students	% of responses (N = 206)
'To explain the gospel/Bible in modern terms'	20%
'To teach the word of God'	20%
'To relate God to our lives'	10%
'To outline rules for living'	8%
'Get across a simple message'	6%

Thus we note a marked similarity between the perceptions of priests and laity in regard to the function of the sermon. Key words were: 'relevant', 'bring God into our lives', 'simple', 'modern' and 'encourage'.

How useful is the sermon?

A general question addressed to the adult laity was: 'How useful, in your experience, is the Sunday sermon in delivering a message to you?' the responses were as follows:

Very Useful/Useful	Useful Sometimes	Not Useful
43.2%	49.5%	7.3%
(N = 183)	(N = 210)	(N = 31)

When the respondents to this question were further examined in regard to their gender, age, marital status, educational qualifications and area of residence, we found the following pattern: the group who responded 'Very Useful/Useful' comprised more of the oldest respondents (65%) than of the youngest (21%), a higher proportion of married (46%) than of single respondents (32%), more people with primary education only (59%), than with second- (33%) or third-level (27%) education, and a higher proportion of rural (43.5%) and small town (55.5%) residents than of those living in city areas (33%). No significant difference was found in the responses of men and women.

We also found that, in general, a higher proportion of the respondents who judged the sermon to be 'Useful' were also those who considered membership of the Catholic Church to be 'Extremely/Very Important'. This group also prayed more frequently and attended Mass and the Sacraments more often than did the group of respondents who were less convinced of the usefulness of the sermon. Thus there was a direct relationship between respondents' 'perceived usefulness' of the sermon, their frequency of prayer, and their attendance at Mass and at the Sacraments.

Additional comments	No. of times mentioned	% of responses
'Only useful when it relates to my life'	47	14.0
'It depends on the way it's delivered'	30	9.0
'It explains how to live a Christian life'	29	8.7
'It depends on the topic'	24	7.2
'I learn some information from it'	22	6.6
'It starts me thinking'	15	4.5
'It helps people understand'	14	4.2
'It doesn't relate to ordinary living'	14	4.2
'It explains the message in the gospel'	13	3.9
'It depends on my mood and willingness to listen'	11	3.3

'Sometimes it's too long to listen to'	9	2.7
'It helps to bring back forgotten beliefs'	9	2.7
'It helps me face the week'	9	2.7
'I don't always understand it'	8	2.4
'Other'	81	24.0
TOTAL	335	100%

The general usefulness of the sermon may be judged from findings in our 1984 National Survey on *Religious Beliefs, Practice and Moral Attitudes*. Respondents were asked to indicate if they would prefer to have the sermon omitted from the Mass. A very large proportion (84%) indicated that they would not like it omitted, while only one in ten (10%) would prefer Mass without a sermon; 6% had no opinion.

Section IV

Evaluation of sermons

Priests were asked whether they had ever asked others to evaluate their sermons. The response pattern was as follows:

Persons consulted

Lay person	52% (N = 115)
Priest + lay person	14% (N = 34)
Priest	12% (N = 32)
All three	15% (N = 26)

The helpfulness of this evaluation was rated as follows:

Very helpful	36% (N = 84)
Helpful	43% (N = 101)
Limited help	18% (N = 42)
Not helpful	2% (N = 5)

Evaluation of sermons by laity

Although more than half of the priests who responded to this survey stated that they had asked a lay person's opinion of a recent sermon, the adults who completed a similar question had not experienced a corresponding degree of consultation. The question to the laity was: 'Have you ever been asked by a priest to give your opinion of his sermon?' The responses were:

Adults		Students	
Yes	No	Yes	No
9%	91%	9%	91%

One suggestion which may explain the discrepancy between the statement of priests and people is that priests may habitually ask the same lay persons, and thus not reach out into the general group of parishioners.

Evaluation of a recent sermon

Although, not unexpectedly, all priests were able to recall the topic of their last sermon, such was not the case with the lay respondents. Almost 50% of the adults and approximately 60% of the students could not recall the topic of the last sermon they had heard.

When asked to assess a recent sermon, the respondents were given certain criteria to be rated. Below is the evaluation of the three groups when asked to judge whether the sermon had been successful in achieving those. It will be noted that the priests are evaluating their own sermons, while the laity are commenting on a recent sermon heard by them. Thus, the groups are not evaluating the same sermons.

Priests' evaluation

Criteria	Very/Fairly Well	Not at all
'It held the people's attention'	92%	0.3%
'It contained some words of encouragement'	91%	1.0%
'It made some reference to Jesus Christ's life'	88%	2.7%
'The sermon made the readings more relevant'	84%	1.5%
'It indicated how Christians should live their daily lives'	81%	0.7%
'It prepared those present to celebrate the Eucharist'	65%	6.3%

'It showed parishioners a way of
living together as a parish
community'   58%   9.2%
'It explained the official teaching
of the Church'   54%   10.8%

When we compared the assessment of these items by the laity,
we found a different pattern of endorsement:

Adults' and students' evaluation

	Very/Fairly Well	
Criteria	Adults	Students
'It indicated how Catholic Christians should live their daily lives'	78%	*
'It made some reference to Jesus Christ's life'	78%	*
'It contained some words of encouragement'	76%	59%
'The sermon made the readings more relevant'	76%	54%
'It explained the official teaching of the Church'	72%	*
'It held the people's attention (in general)'	71%	*
'It showed parishioners a way of living together as a parish community'	65%	*
'It prepared all present to celebrate the Eucharist'	62%	*

* *Omitted in students' questionnaire.*

Since it was not possible to make a direct comparison between
priests and people in any one parish, we make merely a general
comment: higher proportions of priests than of laity gave a
positive assessment of certain key objectives of a recent Sunday
sermon.

Section V

Qualities of a 'good sermon'

All respondents were asked to list some of the most important qualities of a good sermon. We reproduce below[3] the responses given by substantial percentages of priests and laity. It will be noted that the emphases are similar for the three groups:

Priests	% of responses (N=425)
'Brief...reasonably short... not too long'	59%
'Clear and simple...to the point'	52%
'Relevant to the people's lives'	46%
'Encouraging...give hope to the people'	41%

Adults	% of responses (N=399)
'Short'	47%
'To the point'	45%
'Interesting'	41%
'Relevant to everyday life'	22%
'Loud and clearly spoken'	22%

[3]In this, and some subsequent tables, the total percentage is greater than 100% since respondents were given the opportunity of listing up to three desirable qualities.

Students	% of responses (N = 207)
'Short...not too long'	60%
'Interesting'	57%
'Relevant to everyday living...topical'	33%
'Straight to the point'	29%

Preferred length of sermon

Approximately nine in every ten priests preferred a sermon of 5-10 minutes duration. The corresponding percentages for the adults and students were 67% and 56% respectively.

Priests:	6-9	minutes	48%	
	5	minutes	23%	90%
	10	minutes	19%	
Adults:	2-5	minutes	16%	
	6-10	minutes	42%	58%
	11-15	minutes	22%	
Students:	5	minutes	14%	
	10	minutes	36%	50%
	15	minutes	12%	

When priests were asked if and why they chose a longer time than their stated ideal, their reasons were varied. The four main groupings mentioned by a small minority were:

1. 'Depends on the subject...if it's a hobby horse'...'Something I feel strongly about'
2. 'On special occasions only'...'Holy Hours, weddings, Temperance Sunday'...'No heating in church'...'Shared homily'
3. 'If I ramble on and forget the time'
4. 'When poorly prepared'

Omission of sermon

Priests were asked 'Do you ever omit the sermon?' Seventy-two percent answered 'No'; among the remaining 28% the highest proportion was among (a) the younger priests and (b) those working in rural parishes.

Most favoured topics

When asked to name the sermon topics most favoured by them, the priests and laity mentioned the following (smaller percentages were omitted):

Priests:	% of responses (N = 425)
'Mass, Sacraments, Eucharist'	23%
'God's love for us'	20%
'Prayer'	13%
'Justice'	11%

Adults:	% of responses (N = 391)
'God's life'	13%
'Family life'	12%
'Reference to daily life'	12%
'Our Lady'	11%

Students:	% of responses (N = 207)
'Stories related to readings'	13%
'Young people'	12%
'Problems of life'	12%
'Church teaching on current topics'	11%

Attention is tentatively drawn to one divergence in the above pattern: the level of concreteness preferred by the students, by comparison with the more abstract and 'spiritual' topics preferred by priests and adults.

Least favoured topics

The topics most 'disliked' by the three groups were as follows:

Priests:	% of responses (N = 425)
'Sexuality...especially contraception'	77%
'Money...Church finance'	32%
'Controversial subjects'	11%
'Divorce'	5%
'Hell and the Devil'	4%
'Justice'	4%

Adults:	% of responses (N = 428)
'Appeals for money'	29%
'Politics'	25%
'Sex'	9%

Students:	% of responses (N = 207)
'Money...fundraising'	20%
'Sexuality...pre-marital sex'	13%
'Abuse of substances...alcohol, drugs, etc.'	11%

'Disliked' topics common to all three groups were 'Sexuality' and 'Money'.

Section VI

Sermon preparation

Importance

Priests were asked about the importance they attributed to preparation of sermons. Approximately half used the category 'Very important':

Very important	51% (N=211)
Important among other things	48% (N=202)

Age differences

When analysed by age, it was found that proportionately fewer of the younger priests than those in the middle and older age groups used the category 'Very important' (38%, 47% and 69% respectively).

No significant difference was found when the responses were analysed according to location of priests' parishes.

Time spent on sermon preparation

Up to 1 hour	8.8% (N= 33)
1-2 hours	39.5% (N=149)
2-3 hours	18.8% (N= 71)
3-10 hours	15.0% (N= 56)
Throughout the week	18.0% (N= 68)

Selection of topics

Almost two thirds of the priests stated that they followed a pattern of selecting topics for their sermons. These sources were as follows:

Readings of Mass and gospel	62% (N = 262)
Diocesan set themes	7% (N = 31)
Talking with people	4% (N = 19)

Readings

A general question asked whether the priests had read certain resource materials. The following list indicates the pattern:

	% of priests who responded 'Yes'
General Introduction to the Roman Missal	75% (N = 296)
Rite of Christian Initiation of Adults	35% (N = 114)
Introduction to the Lectionary (1981)	50% (N = 172)
Fulfilled in Your Hearing	15% (N = 45)
Directory on Children's Masses	63% (N = 239)

The extent to which priests had read any of the items listed did not vary significantly when the responses were analysed by the priests' age or parish location.

Other written sources were used 'Frequently', with the following variation:

	% of total responses (N = 425)
Scripture in Church	29%
Flor McCarthy's *ABC* series	23%
The Furrow	22%
Intercom	20%
Scripture commentaries	13%
The Living Word	11%

Kevin O'Sullivan's *Sunday Readings*   10%
William Barclay's *Daily Study*
   Bible series   8%
Newspapers   7%

Readings at Mass as a basis for the sermon

The following table shows the frequency with which certain readings or parts of the Mass served as a basis for the sermon:

Item	Often	Sometimes	Rarely/Never
First reading	26%	42%	32%
Second reading	13%	56%	30%
Gospel	96%	3%	0.5%
All three above	33%	41%	25%
Prayers of the Mass	6%	29%	85%
Other parts of Mass	5%	33%	62%
Missalette	9%	9%	82%

Section VII

Consultation

Consultation with others

Priests were asked to indicate the frequency with which they consulted others in preparing their sermons. Their responses were:

Persons consulted	Usually/Sometimes	Rarely/Never
Fellow clergy	42%	58%
Other religious	7%	93%
Groups of laity	22%	78%

When the above responses were analysed by age and by geographical location of parishes, we found the following:

Consultation with fellow clergy

Young (24-40 years) and middle aged priests (41-60 years) were more likely than the older group to say that they 'Usually/Sometimes' consult their fellow clergy in the preparation of their weekly sermon (49%, 46% and 27% respectively).

Clergy in rural areas were less likely to engage in such consultation than were those in urban areas.

Consultation with members of religious orders

When analysed by priests' age, and by location of parish, no significant difference was found in the extent of consultation by priests with religious.

Consultation with groups of laity

Consultation with groups of laity was carried on much more often by the younger priests than by their older counterparts: 32% of the youngest group said 'Usually/Sometimes', compared with 21% of the middle group and 12% of the oldest group.

The helpfulness of the above consultation was rated as follows:

Persons consulted	Very/Fairly helpful	Not helpful
Fellow clergy	90%	10%
Other religious	75%	25%
Groups of laity	90%	10%

When the above responses were analysed by age and by geographical location of parishes, we found the following:

Consultation with fellow clergy

Approximately one third of each age group found consultation with fellow clergy to be 'Very helpful'. A greater proportion (21%) of the oldest group found this process 'Not helpful', compared with 8% of the middle age group (41-60 years) and 6% of youngest (24-40 years) group.

No significant difference emerged when the responses were analysed by location of parish.

Consultation with religious

Proportionately more of the younger priests found it helpful to consult with religious than was the case with the middle and oldest age groups of priests.

No significant difference emerged when the responses were analysed by location of the priests' parishes.

Consultation with groups of laity

Effectiveness of consultation with groups of laity did not differ in regard either to age of priests or to location of their parishes.

Consultation with parish groups

Fewer than a third of the priests had consulted a parish group about the readings for the Mass. Of the 70% who had not, some made the following comments:

Comments	% of those who responded 'No' (N = 288)
'Not yet, but hopefully in the future'	13%
'No suitable group exists in this parish'	7%
'People are not interested... difficult to get even one reader, never mind a group'	6%
'Up to myself to prepare... the laity have no role in the preparation'	6%
'Limitations of time... too busy'	3%
'I frequently discuss them with individuals in an informal manner...nothing organised'	3%

The younger priests met with parish groups more often than did their older colleagues. However, this pattern may have been due, at least in part, to the fact that meeting parish groups for liturgical purposes is often the duty of the more junior curates.

When the responses were analysed by the location of the priests' parishes, we found a variation which corresponded to population density: the more populated the area, the more frequent was the consultation.

Laity's willingness to be consulted

When we examined the laity's attitude towards helping the priests in preparing readings/sermons, we found the students to be more confident than were the adults. The question was: 'Are there any ways in which you would like to help the priest in the task of preaching?' The responses to this question were as follows:

Adults		Students	
Yes	No	Yes	No
17%	82%	53%	47%

Comments by adults:	No. of times mentioned	% of responses (N=73)
'Tell the priest what needs to be discussed'	25	34%
'Give my views to priest'	15	20.5%
'Priest should have meetings with interested parties'	14	19%
'Constructive criticism'	11	15%
'Help the priest prepare the sermon'	11	15%

Comments by students:	No. of times mentioned	% of responses
'Ask the priest to preach' on certain topics'	25	23%
'Speak our own thoughts and ideas'	22	20.5%
'Tell him to use his everyday experiences'	15	14%
'Look interested... give encouragement... thank him'	14	13%
'Help with the readings'	9	8%

Section VIII

Sermon techniques

The three groups were questioned about the effectiveness of certain sermon techniques. Below are the percentages of responses which indicated that the technique was 'very effective'.

Priests	**Very Effective** % of responses (N=425)
'A clear message'	69%
'Reference to the experience of the people listening'	45%
'Use of a story'	42.5%
'Reference to your own personal experience'	37%

Adults:	% of responses (N=428)
'A clear message'	64%
'Use of a story'	40%
'Reference to preacher's own experience'	38%
'Reference to the experience of the people listening'	25%

Students:	% of responses (N = 207)
'A clear message'	32%
'Use of a story'	44%
'Reference to preacher's own experience'	31%
'Reference to the experience of the people listening'	23%

It is clear that the lay respondents favoured 'a story' and 'reference to the priest's experience', whereas the reverse was true in the choices made by priests' assessment of the effectiveness of these techniques.

Use of notes

Priests were asked about various methods of using sermon notes:

In preaching do you...	Yes (N = 425)	No
Use a full written script from which you read?	19%	81%
Use a full written script to which you refer?	50%	50%
Use notes to which you refer?	76%	24%
Prepare notes, but do not refer to them?	64%	36%
Speak without any prior preparation?	15%	85%

When we analysed the above responses in the priests' group by age, we found the following pattern:

1. 'Use a full written script from which you read'
The younger priests were more likely than their older counterparts to read from a script, i.e. 31% of 24-40-year-olds, compared with 17% of 41-60-year-olds and 13.5% of 61-88-year-olds.

2. 'Use a full written script to which you refer'
The younger priests were also more likely than their older counterparts to refer to scripts (57%, 49% and 45% respectively).

3. 'Use notes to which you refer'
Younger priests used notes more often than did the other groups, (82%, 77% and 69% respectively).

4. 'Prepare notes but do not refer to them'
This practice of preparing notes but not referring to them was less common among younger priests than among the older group (58%, 63% and 70% respectively).

5. 'Speak without any prior preparation'
The younger priests were more likely to speak without prior preparation than were their older counterparts, i.e. 24% of 24-40-year-olds, 17% of 41-60-year-olds and 6% of 61-88-year-olds.

Thus, by comparison with the older priests, proportionately more of the younger men (a) read or referred to scripts or notes, (b) spoke without prior preparation.

Section IX

Use of innovative techniques

An attempt was made to ascertain the 'readiness' of priests and people to use creative methods of supporting the message of the sermon at Mass, for example by using liturgical dance, mime or visual aids. The following pattern shows the greater 'openness' of priests and students by comparison with the uncertainty of lay adults:

	Yes	Sometimes	No
Priests:			
Dance	9%	31%	59%
Mime	16%	35%	49%
Visual Aids	35%	35%	30%

	Frequently	Sometimes	Never
Adults:			
Dance	6%	20%	74%
Mime	6%	28%	66%
Visual Aids	15%	37%	48%

	Frequently	Sometimes	Never
Students:			
Dance	11%	35%	53%
Mime	14%	40%	45%
Visual Aids	27%	41%	32%

Comments made by priests and laity

A. Liturgical dance

Priests:	% of total (N=425)
'On special occasions — sometimes useful'	13%
'Distracting...gimmick'	12%
'It would not appeal to ordinary country people'... 'Not part of our culture'	11%
'It must be of a very high standard'	11%

Adults:	% of total (N=319)
'Too distracting'	18%
'It would make Mass more interesting'	15%
'Not suitable for a church'	12%
'Not relevant to Mass'	10%

Students:	% of total (N=207)
'It would make the sermon more interesting and lively'	31%
'It's not a good idea'	13%
'It would look ridiculous'	8%
'It would be too distracting'	6%

B. Mime

Priests:	% of total (N=425)
'Special occasions...sometimes useful'	12%
'It must be of a very high standard'	12%
'Distracting'	8%
'It would not appeal to ordinary country people'	8%

Adults:	% of total (N = 276)
'Not suitable for church'	16%
'Too distracting'	14%
'Helpful in conveying meaning'	12%
'Interesting'	9%

Students:	% of total (N = 173)
'It would be good for illustrating messages'	17%
'Interesting for some Bible stories'	16%
'Boring'	9%
'Ridiculous'	6%

C. Visual aids

Priests:	% of total (N = 427)
'Sometimes useful'	9%
'We live in a visual age... people are used to TV, videos etc.'	8%
'Lasting impression...better than words only'	6%
'Distracting'	6%

Adults:	% of total (N = 270)
'They would assist in understanding'	19%
'They would help gain interest'	14%
'Distracting'	11%
'It would not suit church'	10%

Students:	% of total (N = 207)
'It could make messages clearer'	26%
'Sometimes interesting'	10%
'Could be an improvement'	7%
'It would take attention away from the sermon'	6%

Age and location differences

When we analysed the responses of the priests by age and location of parish we found the following differences:

Liturgical dance

Proportionately more of the younger than the older priests saw an advantage in using liturgical dance to illustrate the sermon (52% of the youngest group, 46% of those aged 41-60 and 22% of the oldest group).

When analysed by location of parish, the responses indicated that priests living in rural areas were less inclined to believe in the usefulness of liturgical dance than were clergy in urban areas.

Mime

The difference of opinion between the three age groups was even more significant in relation to mime. Approximately two thirds (67%) of the youngest group said 'Yes/Sometimes' to the use of mime, compared with 58.5% of the 'middle' group and 25% of the oldest group.

Priests based in rural parishes were generally less favourably disposed towards the use of mime than were urban and suburban priests.

Visual aids to illustrate the sermon

Priests in the young and 'middle' age categories were significantly more in favour of using visual aids to illustrate the sermon than were those in the oldest group, i.e. 80% of the 24-40-year-olds, 78.5% of the 41-60-year-olds and 43% of the 61+ year-olds.

When analysed by geographical location, no significant difference was found between the attitudes of rural or urban-based priests.

Sermons preached by person other than the principal celebrant

A further question probed the readiness of priests to ask others (religious, other priests, laity) to preach at Mass: 'Would you like to have sermons preached by people other than the priest?'. The responses were:

Yes/Sometimes	74%
No	20%
Don't know	6%

The three groups were asked whether they would approve of the sermon being preached by someone other than the celebrant, for example lay persons, sisters, etc. As can be seen from the following pattern, a high percentage were in favour of 'Usually/Sometimes' introducing this innovation.

Priests' responses (N = 234)	Usually/* Sometimes	Rarely	Never
Lay person	81%	14%	5%
Sister	80%	17%	3%
Brother	82%	15%	3%
Visiting priest	93%	6%	1%

Adults' responses
(N = 182)

Lay person	66%	12%	22%
Sister	63%	21%	16%
Brother	69%	19%	12%
Visiting priest	90%	7%	3%

Students' responses
(N = 166)

Lay person	72%	14%	14%
Sister	50%	32%	18%
Brother	55%	32%	13%
Visiting priest	88%	8%	4%

* The percentages are components of those who responded 'Yes' or 'Sometimes'.

The younger priests were more open to the possibility of alternative preachers than were their older colleagues; (84%, 80% and 56% respectively) used the categories 'Yes' or 'Sometimes'.

The younger the priests, the more likely they were to approve of lay people preaching the sermon: 92%, 83% and 65% respectively of the three age groups would 'Usually or Sometimes' like to have sermons given by lay people.

When the responses were analysed by age of priests or location of parishes, no differences in preference were shown for inviting sisters, brothers or visiting priests.

Advice to preachers

The adults and students were asked for three pieces of advice they would like to offer priests in order to improve sermons. The most frequently mentioned were:

Adults:	No. of times mentioned	% of responses (N = 357)
'Keep it short'	130	36%
'Speak clearly — get training if necessary'	70	20%
'Keep to the point'	66	18.5%
'Prepare the sermon well'	54	15%
'Relate the sermon to everyday life'	50	14%

Students:	No. of times mentioned	% of responses (N = 487)
'Be brief...don't drag on'	84	41%
'Make it interesting'	62	30%
'Refer to the everyday experiences of the congregation'	36	17%
'Make the sermon more to the point'	34	16%
'Make it more humorous'	28	13.5%

Section X

Perceived difficulties with sermons

Priests' attitudes to preaching

When asked if they found satisfaction in preaching, the priests' responses were:

Usually	65%
Sometimes	31%
Never	4%

The younger priests 'Usually' found less satisfaction in preaching at Mass than did their older colleagues, i.e., 60% of the 24-40-year-olds, 62% of the middle group and 75.5% of the oldest priests 'Usually' found it satisfactory.

Change in attitude over the last ten years

Almost three quarters of the priests agreed that their attitude towards preaching had changed over the last ten years.

Priests' comments	% of priests who said 'Yes' (N = 294)
'I am now more convinced of its primary importance'	20%

'I am more relaxed now...confident...
   it's nice to hear people laugh'   13%
'I am less forceful and more sensitive to
   people's needs...I speak to people and no
   longer at them'   12%

Almost six in ten priests felt that preaching was more difficult
at present than ten years ago:

More difficult	59%
Less difficult	13%
No difference	28%

No significant difference was found in the replies to this question
when analysed by priests' age or by parish location.

Specific difficulties experienced in preaching

% of responses
(N = 350)

'The variety in the Sunday congregation...
   identifying with all ages and people with
   different educational backgrounds in the
   one sermon'   20%
'Finding resource material...new ideas are
   difficult to find...originality'   19%
'People don't appear to listen...apathy to
   Word of God'   18%
'Fresh presentation for unchanging
   message...preaching to the same people
   every Sunday'   17%
'Making it relevant...identifying with
   marginal groups...unemployed...infrequent
   attenders'   13%

Conclusion

1. *Perceptions of preaching*

    One important finding of our research is that while 43% of the adult laity found the Sunday sermon 'Generally useful', 57% found it either 'Occasionally useful' or 'Of no use at all'. This pattern suggests a substantial level of dissatisfaction with the current standard of preaching in Sunday liturgy. It may help to explain why 50% of the adults and 60% of students could not recall the topic preached on the previous Sunday. On the other hand, it is clear that this dissatisfaction does not arise from a lack of interest in the word of God expounded by the celebrant or his minister. The overwhelming majority of the laity (84%) want to hear a sermon when they attend Mass. In other words, there is a certain hunger for the word of God which is not being satisfied.

    The 57% who were less than satisfied with the usefulness of the Sunday sermon comprised proportionately more of the youngest (under 40) respondents, of single persons, of those with higher levels of education and city dwellers. No significant difference was found between the opinions of men and women.

    The laity leave little doubt as to the kind of homily they wish to hear: one which is well-prepared, brief, to the point, with a simple message, well-delivered, one which makes the gospel message relevant to their lives, which offers encouragement in following the Lord, and which encourages growth of community and animates the current celebration of the Eucharist. It seems safe to assume that when too many of these qualities are missing, heads nod and other interests take over.

2. Consultation and evaluation

Substantial numbers of priests had neither discussed the readings with others, nor asked for evaluation of the sermon. However, of those who had requested evaluation, 90% had found it helpful.

Perhaps the reluctance to ask for evaluation may explain the 'mis-match' between the priests' and laity's assessment of the success of sermons. On the whole, higher percentages of priests than of laity expressed confidence that sermons met certain criteria of 'success'.

3. Training of preachers

Less than half the priests (48%) were satisfied with seminary training for preaching, either in regard to content or to method. This was true of all age groups and localities. On the other hand, 57% now felt themselves adequately equipped for this ministry, largely, it was said, due to learning from their own experience.

Only 40% had attended post-ordination courses in preaching, but of these, the vast majority (80%) found them helpful. Almost two thirds (64%) expressed a wish for further training.

4. Resources for preaching ministry

More than two-thirds of the priests favoured a preaching resource centre, located preferably in their own diocese. Facilities mentioned included a library of books, periodicals, tapes and videos as well as resource persons and equipment.

5. *Importance of preaching*

   Both clergy and laity recognise the importance of preaching. More than 90% of the clergy rated it as 'Important' or 'Very important', while 84% of the laity want a homily with their Sunday Mass.

6. *Function of preaching*

   There exists a marked similarity between the perceptions of priests and laity in regard to the function of the sermon. Key phrases were:

Priests:	'Instruct...educate...explain' (25%)
Adults:	'Explain the readings in everyday language' (16%)
Students:	'Explain the gospel/Bible in modern terms' (20%)

   Further examination of these replies suggest a joint concern to make a definite link between the biblical message and life as experienced today.

7. *Preparation of sermons*

   About two thirds of the clergy spend 1-3 hours preparing their homilies (this includes 15% 'throughout the week'), 15% spend 4 or more hours.
   Topics are usually chosen from the gospel reading (62%). Resources used are mainly written texts, *Scripture in Church* in first place (29%). Some priests occasionally consult beforehand with fellow clergy (42%), fewer consult with laity (22%). Those who did consult however, found it helpful (90%).
   In addition, at least some of the laity are available to assist in this process: 17% of adults and 53% of students said they were ready to help.

8. *Delivery*

   There is a remarkable consensus among priests and laity, young and adult concerning preaching style. Homilies should be brief, clear, interpret the word of God by applying it to life. According to the laity, to do this preachers should draw on their own experience. Otherwise they should draw on that of their people — to bring home the message. Storytelling was rated highly as part of this approach.

9. *Difficulties in preaching*

While most priests find satisfaction in the ministry of the word, many are conscious of difficulties arising from changing conditions of culture and faith. They note in particular: variety in the Sunday congregation; demand for originality; presence of marginalised groups; indifference on the part of some; sensitive topics such as money, sex, politics and justice; reaching the young.

10. *The readings*

Among the laity, adult and young, the message of the gospel reading was most significant (adults; 52% 'get a lot from the gospel', another 40% 'got something'; 32% of youth 'get a lot from the gospel', another 41% 'get something'); difficulty is experienced with the other readings. This may be partly explained by the fact that most have no recollection of the liturgy of the word having been explained to them (87% adults; 95% youth). On the other hand the great majority would welcome such explanation, as well as short introductions to the readings, with competent lectors called for to present the message. Little study is made of the lectionary apart from Mass itself: 20% of adults read the lessons in advance; 7% study them after Mass; even fewer young people do so.

11. *Acceptance of alternative preachers*

Priests and students were the groups most open to admitting 'preachers' other than the celebrant (lay persons, sisters, etc.). Most favoured persons were a visiting priest, a religious brother, a lay person, a religious sister — in that order of preference.

125

12. *Younger age groups*

In many cases the data revealed substantial differences on the basis of age. Younger priests differed substantially from middle or older groups. A similar pattern was found among adults, where attitudes of the youngest adults approximated to those of the students. Thus, one final emphasis of the survey highlights the special needs of the younger groups, both priests and laity.